YOU CAN GO THE DISTANCE

MARATHON TRAINING GUIDE: ADVICE, PLANS & MOTIVATION FOR ALL RUNNERS

YOU CAN GO THE DISTANCE

MARATHON TRAINING GUIDE: ADVICE, PLANS & MOTIVATION FOR ALL RUNNERS

Bruce Van Horn

www.YouCanGoTheDistance.com

COPYRIGHT

*"Let us run with endurance
the race that is set before us."*
— Hebrews 12:1

"Life is a Marathon, so let's train for it!"
— Bruce Van Horn

Table of Contents

Testimonials 9

Not JUST a Marathon Training Book..................................11

Not JUST a Book!..15

Caitlyn's Story 17

First Things First: Set a Goal...25

Choose the Right Plan..31

Build a Strong Foundation 37

Train in ALL Conditions 43

Let's Talk Cross-Training 51

Yasso 800s: Speed + Endurance......................................55

Tempo Runs 61

The Long Run: You CAN Go the Distance! 65

Long Run Recovery 75

Develop a Race-Day Routine, Now!..................................81

Roll with the Changes!...89

Time for a Progress Check 93

Rock Lobster Running 99

Is it Time for New Shoes? 105

Proper Running Form..111

Nutrition: Choose the Right Fuels! 119

Let the Taper Begin!..139

Ready or Not, It's GO Time! 145

The Finish Line! 151

About the Author 159

The YCGTD Training Plan.................................161

Testimonials

Bruce, I love the chapter! I feel honored that you would include Yasso 800s in your book!

— Bart Yasso, CRO, Runner's World

Bruce Van Horn understands the new world of engagement better than anyone I know. He is constantly uplifting and coaching others. He is always available, helping others get over their plateaus, and move to the next level. Bruce will help take "can't" out of your vocabulary and replace it with "CAN." He constantly puts out value into the world which makes the world a much better place.

— J.B. Glossinger, MBA, PhD
CEO & Founder, MorningCoach.com
& Alive Foundation

Bruce helped us start and coached our middle school cross-country team at GCA. He motivated our kids to reach goals that they thought were unreachable. By the end of the first season, they were working together as a team, helping and encouraging each other as Bruce taught them. GCA benefits to this present day from Bruce's motivation and leadership.

— Doug Dillon, Athletic Director
Guardian Christian Academy

Bruce, this was exactly what I needed today. I'm training for Richmond too! This will be my 2nd 26.2 and I'm hoping to break 4:30. I had heard about Yasso 800s but have never tried them. I'm going out tomorrow to give it a try. Thanks! — Cathy G.

Bruce, this was most helpful, thanks! I've only run 10Ks up to now, but a friend of mine has been trying to talk me into a marathon. I think I'm ready to try it! — Pete A

Bruce, your advice/warning on over striding helped me identify my problem which was causing hip/back pain. Who would have thought the wrong stride would have caused all that pain. Thanks! — Heidi D.

Bruce, I'm thinking about running my first marathon, I'm loving your message to beginners. — Carlos A

Not JUST a Marathon Training Book

You might be thinking, "Another book about Marathon training? Seriously?"

I know there are a lot of books already written about Marathon training. I've read many of them and some of them are very comprehensive, and some are written by world-class runners and well-known coaches. So what in the world could Bruce Van Horn have to say about Marathon training that hasn't already been said or that would add value to you, the reader?

I thought the very same thing! However, through the persistence of several friends, many of my blog readers, and Twitter and Facebook followers who encouraged me to write this book, I started to rethink the idea. I realized that what I have to say on the subject is a bit different than the other books on the market. My story, my experiences, and the way I've been able to use those experiences to encourage and motivate others to reach their goals are ways for me to add value. That is my only motivation: To add value to your life and be a source of encouragement to give you the confidence to reach your goals!

What I want to share with you is not so much about training your body—though that is important and I cover a lot of that in this book. The most import part of marathon training, however, is training your mind! It is about removing the word "can't" from your vocabulary.

If you are already a marathon runner, I think there is still value here for you, as well. Many of the workouts and tips I share with you are not just for beginners, but can be used to help intermediate runners improve their performance.

If you have never run a marathon before, but maybe have it on your "Bucket List," I know what's holding you back. I know because I have been there. It's fear. Fear of the distance and fear of failure. I won't lie to you, 26.2 miles is a long distance to run! You're thinking, "There's no way I could ever run that far!"

I know because I said those exact words to my older brother, who was a marathon runner, when he told me I should try it. I thought he was crazy… but I was wrong!

Most people never run a marathon, or quit trying a few weeks into their training, because they convince themselves they can't do it.

What I learned about myself, and what I am going to help you learn about yourself, is that you CAN go the distance!

My brother's words echoed in my head for a few weeks. I was overweight, out of shape, and had not run since high school. I decided the least I could do is start exercising and do some light jogging. It took me over a month to get to the point I could jog one mile without walking. But reaching that milestone gave me a boost of confidence. One mile became two, and two became three and, less than a year later, I completed my first marathon!

I also want to tell you that fear is a lie! I have seen it as the acronym: F.E.A.R. = False Evidence Appearing Real

I struggled with fear and self-doubt for a long time. Fortunately, someone pushed me out of my comfort zone and encouraged me to at least try. Once I decided to at least try, the fear and doubt gradually faded away.

So, while this IS a book about marathon training, it's not JUST a book about marathon training!

In this book, I am going to help you learn how to change the way you think about your goals and the challenges you will face in life. I will give you the confidence to believe in yourself and help you find the courage to conquer fear and take the first steps toward achieving those goals and doing the things you never thought you could do.

I do not want to just be your coach. I will be your cheerleader, your biggest fan, and the friend who is going to push you—when you need a little push—to get out of your comfort zone and on your way to being a marathon runner!

So I will tell you again; **you CAN go the distance!**

Let's get started!

Not JUST a Book!

"You CAN Go the Distance!" is not JUST a book that you read once and then put aside. I've written this book with the hope that you will use it as a reference to look back upon as you move through your training and as a source of inspiration and motivation. Throughout this book, I will tell you and show you "You CAN!"

In addition to the book, however, I have also created a website, **www.YouCanGoTheDistance.com**, to be an on-line resource and community for you. On the website, you find the complete text for some chapters and partial text for other chapters in this book. You'll be able to interact with other readers and me by posting comments or questions in each chapter.

There are also how-to and motivational videos, and links to other on-line resources.

My goal with the book and the website is to give you the confidence of knowing you are not in this alone. Marathon runners are a very generous and helpful breed of people, so they will be there to support you and answer your questions too!

When you get to the last chapter, The Finish Line, be sure to jump over to that section of the website. When you finish your marathon, or any other race or big accomplishment, tell us about it at The Finish Line **www.YouCanGoTheDistance.com/book/ finish-line** so we can cheer for you and give you a virtual High-Five. Also, come see who else has finished their race and be a cheerleader for them.

As you read through this book, if you have any questions, want to share a comment, or otherwise engage with the community, just go to the corresponding chapter at:

www.YouCanGoTheDistance.com/book

You can also interact with me and others through Twitter and Facebook. Join our social community at:

Twitter:
www.twitter.com/YouCanGoTheDist

Facebook:
www.facebook.com/YouCanGoTheDistance

Caitlyn's Story

Caitlyn was a very cute, outgoing, but slightly over-weight, 6th grade girl, who very much wanted to be on the Middle School Cross Country team. Her primary motivation for wanting to be a part of the team, as is the motivation for many young people, was because many of her friends were going to be on the team.

Caitlyn had a problem, though. It's called self-doubt. She had never been very athletic, and because of her weight, she was convinced that she would never be able to run the entire 3.1 mile course. How do I know that? She told me!

Just before the first practice of the season, she pulled me aside and said "Coach Van Horn, I'm really scared. I want to do this, but I know I'll never be able to run that far. I've never done it before."

"Have you ever tried?" I asked her.

"No," she said looking at the ground and with a slight quiver in her voice.

"Then how do you know you can't do it?" I countered.

"I just know I can't." She said, moving some dirt with her foot.

I put my arm gently on her shoulder and said "Caitlyn, you've already done the hardest part."

She looked up at me, incredulously, and said "What…?"

"This might sound strange, Caitlyn, but the hardest part of doing anything new, is finding the courage and making the decision to actually try it! You're here, you're dressed in your running clothes, and you've told me you really want to do this. You've already done the hardest part."

I don't think she believed me, but we walked over to where the rest of the team had gathered near the front of the school. I talked with the kids about Cross Country running and explained that, today, we would go out to learn the course. They could run, jog, walk, at any pace they wanted, but we would go the full distance of the course.

As we all started out, I asked Caitlyn to stay with me and told her we would run the course together. I told her I would stay with her the whole way and that it didn't matter how fast or slow we went, so there was no pressure.

As is typical for most kids—most runners, in fact—some of the pack went out really fast and got far out ahead of Caitlyn and me.

"See, look at them," she said. "I'll never be able to keep up with them."

I just smiled to myself and said "Don't worry about them. Let's just do the best we can and see what you can do."

Did I mention that Caitlyn loved to talk? Did she ever! As we jogged, she started talking much faster than her feet were moving. She talked to me about all the things she liked to do, about her family, about school and her friends, the music she likes, etc. I was listening to her, but not saying anything in response. Just the occasional "yep, oh, that's cool."

As we were jogging and she was talking, I was noticing something that she didn't and I wasn't about to point out to her. She just kept talking and she just kept jogging…

What was happening was this: while she was completely caught up in whatever story she was telling me, we were passing other kids who were now walking and out of breath. We just jogged right past them and she did not even notice! Some of the kids we passed were the same kids who had gone out in that initial fast pack—the same kids she said she could never keep up with!

Eventually, we came to a spot near the front of the school where several runners had stopped and were talking and drinking water. Caitlyn was still talking…

With a slight smirk on my face, I said "OK, let's stop now, Caitlyn. Go ahead and get some water."

"Oh, OK" she said, smiling, and walked over to the water cooler to get a cup of water.

More kids had come up behind us and were gathering with our group. They were drinking and talking and giving each other fist-bumps and high-fives while still catching their breaths.

After she had had a few cups of water, I asked Caitlyn to come over to me.

I put my arm around her sweaty shoulders and said with a mock-serious voice, "Do you know what you just did, Caitlyn?"

"What… No, what did I do?" she said with a look of concern on her face.

"You just did what you said you could NEVER do! You just ran the entire course. You just ran 3.1 miles!"

"WHAAATTTT?!!!!" she gasped, putting her hands up to her mouth in shock.

"That's right! You were so busy talking…" I winked at her, "that you didn't even notice that you were running… or that you never stopped to walk… or that you passed about half of these other kids!"

She just started jumping up and down with her hands still over her mouth. For the first time, maybe in her entire life, she was unable to speak! She had tears running down her cheeks and wrapped her arms around me and hugged me tight.

"Thank you, thank you, thank you!!" she said, looking up at me with tears still in her eyes.

"You don't need to thank me," I said, ruffling her already tangled hair. "You're the one who did it. All I did was believe in you!"

You see, all of life's treasures are guarded by fear and self-doubt.

The hardest part of doing anything new is finding the courage to decide to at least try. Confidence is something that only comes with experience. It's OK to be scared. Do it scared. It's OK to doubt your ability. Do it with doubt. You'll never know if you can if you don't try.

It makes no sense at all, when you stop to think about it, how we are so afraid of trying something new because we don't think we can do it. Seriously, think about it. We cannot do anything we have never tried before, until we actually try it! We do not know how to do anything until we try to acquire the knowledge and skills needed.

So, I want you to make a few changes to your vocabulary that will, ultimately, make a change in your mindset. I want you to replace the word "can't" with the word "CAN." And if that proves too difficult for you at the start, I want you to add the word "yet" to the end of any sentence that contains the word "can't."

Instead of saying "I can't do that," I want you to start saying "I can't do that, yet!" Instead of "I don't know how," I want you to say "I don't know how, yet!"

If you will do that, if you will at least try, you will soon be saying "Yes, I CAN do it. Yes, I CAN go the distance!"

To leave comments or questions about this chapter on the website, go to this chapter on:
www.YouCanGoTheDistance.com/book

First Things First: Set a Goal

This might seem like a no-brainer, but so many people skip the most important step for achieving anything. You have to know what it is you want to accomplish. You have to set a goal.

It is essential that you set goals in your life. Goals give you something to stay motivated about, a target to aim for, a dream to make real.

I am going to assume, since you are reading this book, that you have already set a goal. You have said to yourself (or you will by the time you finish reading this book), "I want to run a marathon."

"I want to run a marathon," is, indeed, a goal. But it's not a great goal. It is too vague. You need to make it more specific so you can take the necessary steps to achieve that goal.

Saying "I want to run a marathon" is really like saying "I want to be rich." The problem is "rich" means different things to different people and it is too open-ended. It would be better to say "I want to have $100,000 in my bank account." It would be even better to say "I want to have $100,000 in my bank account within the next 5 years." Now that's a goal!

Let us take this same principal and apply it to our marathon goal. Instead of just saying "I want to run a marathon," say something like this: "I want to run a marathon by this time next year and I want to finish it in less than 5 hours."

When you are specific, you are able to break your goal down into actionable steps and can measure your progress along the way.

Set yourself up for success, not for failure!

If you are a hard-driving, high-achieving, motivated person (or want to be one), it is so easy to make a huge mistake at this point. You are probably tempted to set a goal that is too ambitious and you are setting yourself up for failure. Trust me; I've done this more times than I care to admit!

If you set unrealistic goals, those goals can become demotivating instead of being the inspiration that keeps you moving forward. It is very important to set realistic goals, not just for your marathon training but for your overall life, as well.

It can be very motivating to realize half-way through your training that you set a goal that was too easy and to be able to adjust your goal upward at that point. On the flip-side, however, it can be emotionally devastating to have to scale back because you bit off too much to chew from the start.

Do yourself a huge favor and set yourself up for success!

How to Set a Goal:

"I've never run a marathon before, so how can I know what should be a realistic goal?" you ask.

The answer is simple: You set your marathon goal based on some current or previous achievement and extrapolate that result out to a realistic marathon goal. I'll show you how.

I'm a huge fan of Greg McMillan's "Equivalent Effort" calculator. You can find the online calculator here:

www.YouCanGoTheDistance.com/calculator

His calculator is very easy to use and I've found it to be an exceptionally reliable tool. The premise is simple: You take the time of your best race and enter that time and distance into the calculator. Based on that time/distance, the calculator tells you what times you should be able to run for other distances using roughly the same amount of "effort" of your previous race.

For example, if you can run a 10K in 1 hour (60 min), you should be able to run a half marathon in 2hrs 13min, and a full marathon in 4hrs 41min. How cool is that?

The thing I love the most about this tool, is that, if you've run some other distance like a 10K before, it shows you in a very real way that you CAN, in fact, run a marathon. Not only does it show you that you CAN, it shows you how fast you should be able to run it if you put in the training.

You can plug in any known distance and time and it will give you the same "equivalent effort" results.

No matter what, I want you to set a specific goal with a specific finish time!. Don't say "Well, I don't really care how long it takes, I just want to finish." That's just a dream, not a measurable, trainable goal.

Let's do it this way instead: All races have a maximum allowed time before they close the course. For example, the Richmond Marathon has a 7 hour time limit. That's an average 16min per mile pace. So, now, instead of saying "I just want to finish," you can say "I'd like to run the Richmond Marathon next year and finish it in less than 7 hours."

OK, now we have a specific time that we can plug into our calculator and start training to reach that goal. Dreams are just vague wishes. Goals are specific and measurable. Set Goals!

So now you know what to do. Set a goal! Pick something realistic using the McMillan Running Calculator and go for it.

Numbers and Jargon:

Every group of people with similar interests, be they accountants, engineers, nurses or runners, have a kind of language they use, a jargon that you need to get used to. And they all love acronyms! Runners are no different, so here are a few you should learn right away.

When you use the McMillan calculator, or any other tool, to set your race goal, there are two numbers you need to pay attention to.

First, what is your Marathon Goal? This is your overall time in which you plan to run the marathon. Mine is 3:30 (3 hours, 30 minutes). Yours may be 2:45 or 5:30. So just remember this time because I'll reference your Marathon Goal in upcoming chapters.

Second, what is your Race Pace (RP)? This is simply your Marathon Goal broken down into an average Pace Per Mile (PPM). For example, my Marathon Goal is 3:30, which breaks down to an average PPM of 8:01 (8 minutes, 1 second per mile). So my, Race Pace (RP) is 8:01.

Also, as I cover some specific types of running workouts, you'll encounter terms like: Yasso 800s, Tempo Runs, Long Runs, Recovery Runs/Jogs, Tapering, etc.

Don't get too hung up on these if you are confused already. I just want to prepare you for some of the acronyms and jargon that you'll encounter and that I'll used (as sparingly as possible) throughout this book.

To leave comments or questions about this chapter on the website, go to this chapter on:
www.YouCanGoTheDistance.com/book

Choose the Right Plan

Now that you have set a goal for your marathon, it is time to choose a plan to help you achieve that goal.

If you do an Internet search for "marathon training plans," you will get back hundreds, if not thousands, of search results. There are almost as many training plans to choose from as there are actual marathons to run. My recommendation is that you talk to some of your friends and family members who have run marathons before to find out what they use or recommend.

If you live in a large enough city, there are many running groups, clubs, or YMCAs that have training teams. I highly recommend you join one of these teams, if you have that option. There are two very important reasons I make this recommendation:

First, they will be using a training plan and schedule that has been proven to be effective. They may actually have different teams and plans based on experience levels, like beginner, intermediate, and advanced.

Second, being part of a training team adds to the social and accountability aspects of your training. Running with other people of similar ability simply makes running more fun. Also, by being part of a team, you will have a coach, or team leader, and the other runners to hold you accountable to getting in your training runs. Everyone will ask "did you get in your runs this week?" and knowing that in advance will give you the added motivation to make sure you get out of bed to do the work!

An additional benefit to joining a marathon training team is that they will often hold clinics or bring in guest speakers to talk about various topics related to running. They might bring in a local running store owner to talk about the different types of shoes or equipment available, or a Sports Medicine doctor to talk about treating various injuries, etc. This information from experts can really help you with your running.

While I will share with you the training program I've developed over the years, there are two training programs I highly recommend:

Hal Higdon is the "grandfather" of marathon training. Hundreds of thousands of runners have used his training programs for many years. I used his Novice

2 program to train for my first marathon. Hal's programs are tried-and-true and they are also free! You can find all of his marathon training programs here:

www.YouCanGoTheDistance.com/hal-higdon

Runner's World has many training plans to choose from, all of which have been developed by marathon veterans. While they aren't free, they might be worth the price because of the level of detail they give you. If you'd like to check them out, you can do so here:

www.YouCanGoTheDistance.com/RW-Training-Plans

It doesn't really matter to me which plan you choose, but I absolutely do want you to pick a plan and stay with it. The marathon is your destination. A training plan is your road map. Without a plan, you won't reach your destination!

The "You CAN Go the Distance!" plan

I've used many different plans through the years and have found benefits and drawbacks to each of them. Maybe I'm just hard to please, but I haven't found just one plan that was right for me. Consequently, I've taken pieces and parts from the plans that I've used and come up with my own plan. After you've run a few marathons, you might do the same thing to suit your particular running needs and style.

The "You CAN Go the Distance!" (YCGTD from now on) plan only has three running days per week, whereas most other plans have you running four or five days per week. The three runs are very specific types of runs and you'll be cross-training or resting between your running days. This plan also has four 20-mile Long Runs in it, whereas some only have one or two.

The YCGTD plan is 18 weeks long and all of the runs are based on the Marathon Goal you set in the previous chapter. If you haven't set your goal yet, go back to that chapter and do it before you start this program.

The three types of runs used in this plan are:

- Yasso 800s
- Tempo Runs
- Long Runs

I will explain each of these types of runs in their own chapters.

You will find complete instructions and a weekly Training Schedule at the back of this book.

To download a printable training plan worksheet, go here:

www.YouCanGoTheDistance.com/plan

I know you're excited about getting started, but I highly recommend that you read the next chapter, *Build a Strong Foundation*, before you begin. You should also read through the chapter on each specific type of run before you attempt that run.

OK, you have a goal and now you have a plan. Let's get training, using our goal and our plan so that we CAN go the distance!

To leave comments or questions about this chapter on the website, go to this chapter on:
www.YouCanGoTheDistance.com/book

Build a Strong Foundation

Once you come up with a premise, you have to work out how it all happened. It's a bit like coming up with a spectacular roof design first. Before you can get it up there, you need to build a solid foundation and supporting structure.

— Linwood Barclay

You are about to embark on a grand adventure, a marathon (literally) of a journey. You are about to start a training program that will change your body, change your mind, and change your life in many ways. You are about to become a Marathon runner!

Before you start your training plan, however, you need to have a solid foundation upon which to build. A solid foundation is an absolute must in order to assure success.

The obligatory disclaimer. Common sense is becoming a rare commodity, so I am obliged to tell you to consult a physician or other medical professional before you begin any exercise program, especially a marathon training plan! OK? Seriously, if you have any health issues that might get worse as a result of your training, you really want to know that now before anything bad happens. Go see your doctor and tell him/her what you are planning to do and ask if he/she is aware of anything that would be a problem for you as you train.

How many people do you know who have set a New Year resolution to get in better shape? The story is so common it is predictable. You make your resolution and go to a local gym. You are so excited about getting in better shape that you hit it really hard on that first visit—you lift weights, you run on the treadmill, you take an aerobics class—and you feel really good while you are doing it! Right? Right! That is until the next morning when you can't get out of bed or bend over to pull up your pants because you are too sore!

Often, when we get excited about a new exercise program or goal, we go into it thinking we can accomplish anything and we over-do it. Consequently, we are too sore to go back to do it the next day… or the next. Or worse, we hurt ourselves on that first day and we physically can't go back to do it again anytime soon. I don't want this to happen to you!

It is extremely important that you build a strong foundation before you start your marathon training.

I want you to look at the first week of your marathon training program to see what is going to be required of you. Many plans have you running at least 8 miles for the Long Run in the first week. That is exactly what my plan, the YCGTD Marathon Training Plan, requires in Week 1.

If you have never run 8 miles before, I don't want you to even attempt starting Week 1 yet. The last thing I want you to do is start your training program and get frustrated, or injured, and quit!

Also, I want to remind you that you CAN go the distance! So, if you are looking at Week 1 and thinking that you can't go 8 miles, I want you to stop right now and change your thinking. I want you to change the phrase "I can't" to "I can't, yet" and just get started with any distance. Every world-class runner started right where you are now. Deciding to try it and then getting out there and doing it, one step at a time, is how they became world-class. You CAN do this!

I want you to start out short and easy for a few weeks. Short and easy will build the foundational muscles you need, and, more importantly, it will build the foundational confidence you need. Give yourself some small victories at the very beginning. Those small victories will propel you into bigger victories as you grow.

Take however many weeks you need to build up to the point you can go the distance required by Week 1 of your chosen plan.

I also don't want you to be concerned with time… yet. Even if you just walk the 8 miles, that's OK. You are training your brain to go the distance—and that is the most important muscle you need to train! Once you have trained your brain to go the distance, your brain will train your body.

I want you to get to the point that you can do whatever is required by Week 1 of your program for at least two weeks in a row before you officially start your training. If it takes you five weeks to get to the point where you can do your Week 1 requirement, that's fine. In fact, it's more than fine—it's fantastic! It is fantastic because you have stuck it out for five weeks, which means you are committed and already showing signs of mental endurance, and that will serve you well as you train for your marathon.

So, promise me, and promise yourself, that you will start off very easy to avoid injury or frustration and that you will not just jump into Week 1 without having built a strong foundation. A house built on a strong foundation can weather many storms!

To leave comments or questions about this chapter on the website, go to this chapter on:
www.YouCanGoTheDistance.com/book

Train in ALL Conditions

We are what we repeatedly do. Excellence, therefore, is not an act but a habit.

— Aristotle

There are a few places on the globe where the weather is the same almost every day. Unfortunately, I do not live in one of those places.

There are a few people in this world who have very little hardship or stress in their lives. Unfortunately, I do not live one of those lives.

Chances are pretty good that you do not live in one of those places or live one of those lives either!

Sometimes, when you set a goal to start training for something, life happens or weather happens and the training conditions become, shall we say, less than ideal. OK, let's be real—sometimes, the training conditions will just suck!

When it is too hot for the kids to even go to the pool, it is no fun to be out running. When you get up to run at 5:00am and realize that it is pouring rain outside, it is normal to want to crawl right back into bed and hope for better weather tomorrow.

It is rare that you will get a week of absolutely perfect weather or a week of no personal trials. In fact, if you are waiting for those kinds of weeks, you will never train and you will never reach your goal.

Marathon training is like life; it requires that you train in all conditions and for all situations!

We need to train our bodies and our minds in all conditions and for all situations. This will enable us to face the ups and downs and the storms of life with confidence.

www.TimesDispatch.com Richmond Times-Dispatch ● Sunday, November 12, 2006

ALEXA WELCH EDLUND/TIMES-DISPATCH

Bruce Van Horn, 43, of Midlothian ran a 4:01:32 in yesterday's SunTrust Richmond Marathon and then tried to cool off.

Depending on where and when your planned marathon is being held, you probably have no way of knowing what the weather will be like 18 weeks from now. It could be very cold or very hot (like it was in the 2006 Richmond Marathon, see the picture of me above!), or raining, sleeting, etc.… and the conditions can actually change while you're in the middle of the race! You just do not know what you will encounter, so you need to be ready for everything.

When conditions are not what you want them to be, you still need to get out there and do your training. Now, I am not suggesting you go running when there is air-to-ground lightening or when the conditions are otherwise dangerous, but you need to decide whether or not the conditions are dangerous or just inconvenient!

There are two reasons I want you get out and run regardless of the weather: Physical conditioning and Mental conditioning.

Physical Conditioning:

I am always amazed when I go running through my neighborhood in the early morning rain and do not see the runners I normally see if the weather is nice. I ask myself "what are they going to do if it's raining on race day?"

Remember that confidence is only gained through experience, and the only way to gain experience is to have gone through a situation. Come race day, you want to be prepared not just to go the distance, but to go the distance regardless of the conditions!

By running in the rain or in the heat or in the cold, you not only learn how to run in those conditions, you also learn about your shoes and clothes, which is almost just as important! You need to know if those shorts cause chaffing if they get wet, or if your socks cause blisters when your feet get wet or very hot. These things are really important to have worked out prior to your marathon.

Even though I want you to train in adverse conditions, I want you to adjust your expectations with the conditions.

When it is very hot or cold or raining hard, you should not expect to run as fast as you would under ideal conditions. To try to push hard in extreme conditions is just inviting injury, which can totally derail your training plan, so pull back the throttle and slow down. It is OK to slow down, but try not to cut your distances short. A marathon is always 26.2 miles regardless of the weather!

What do you do if the conditions really are dangerous?

If the conditions are dangerous to your safety or health, then, by all means, use common sense and do not go out for a run! I do not want you to crawl back into bed, though, because of the mental conditioning that would cause. Instead of running on that day, switch your schedule around and make this a "Cross-Training" day. You will read about cross-training in the next chapter.

Mental Conditioning:

Throughout this book, I am going to tell you that, in many ways, the marathon is harder mentally than it is physically. You might not agree with me at this point, but once you complete a marathon, you will see I was right. I have a good friend, who has run 58 marathons in his life, and even he agrees with me!

Mental conditioning is arguably more important than physical conditioning because it is the mental conditioning that pushes you to make the right choices to do the physical conditioning.

No matter what you do, you are always training for something! By skipping a run, you are actually training your brain to do that the next time. If you skip your run today because it is raining, it will be easier to skip your run tomorrow if it is still raining. Your brain will tell your body to do what it did the last time. So if you skipped your run today, your brain will tell your body (in just a quiet whisper) that it's OK to skip it tomorrow.

Your physical conditioning is dependent on your ability to stay mentally conditioned!

Inertia can be your best friend or your worst enemy. Remember the definition of inertia? "Inertia is the resistance of any physical object to any change in its motion" or the phrase "a body at rest tends to stay at rest; a body in motion tends to stay in motion."

If you give up every time things do not go according to plan... guess what? You are training your body and your brain to give up every time things do not go according to plan! You are actually training to fail!

So when life happens and things don't go according to plan, don't give up and say "I'll just get out there next week" No! Adjust your plan and your expectations, but keep going! Your body and your brain need to be trained for all conditions.

If you will push yourself out the door when you do not feel like it, you will be happier in the long run (pardon the pun). If you keep doing it, you will get used to it and it will be easier the next time and, eventually, it will not even occur to you that the weather is bad!

You can do this! It takes time and conditioning, but you can do this!

To leave comments or questions about this chapter on the website, go to this chapter on:
www.YouCanGoTheDistance.com/book

Let's Talk Cross-Training

Marathon training does, indeed, require a lot of running, but you should not run every day!

Before I get into some of the specific running workouts for marathon training, I want to talk a bit about cross-training.

There is no magic to cross-training. Cross-training is simply doing some exercise other than running.

Swimming, biking, Pilates, yoga, situps, pushups, planks, squats, upper-body weight lifting, etc, are all great examples of cross-training.

The purpose of cross-training is two-fold. First, it gives your legs and feet a chance to rest and recover.

The marathon training schedule I use, the YCGTD Marathon Training Plan, only has 3 runs per week, but they are very intense and specific types of running workouts (which I will cover in later chapters), and my 50-year-old body needs the recovery time in between runs. Cross-training on the non-running days has been a huge help to me while I recover.

What most beginner athletes do not understand is that strength is actually created during the rest/recovery period rather than the actual training. Recovery is crucial to building strength. This is why you do not want to run every day. You need to give your feet and legs time to recover. Plus, you need to strengthen other parts of your body—marathon run requires your entire body to be in shape, not just your legs!

The second purpose of cross-training is to strengthen other muscle groups that indirectly support your running. For example, swimming helps improve cardio and upper body strength, both of which are important to running. Pilates, yoga, planks, and simple push-ups and sit-ups improve your core strength which you will need for endurance and posture on those long runs.

While I have mentioned biking as a great cross-training exercise, I want you to be careful if you use a bike. Remember that the primary goal of cross-training is to give your legs a break while they recover from running. Biking, whether on a real bike or on a stationary bike, should be done lightly, not as an aggressive workout.

Let me say a word about treadmills. Treadmills can be great as a way to get in a run if the weather is bad, but there is a temptation to use treadmills too often out of convenience, especially in extra cold or extra hot weather conditions. There is, however, no substitute for road running. Your marathon will not be run on a treadmill; it will be run on the road!

The other problem is that people do not use treadmills properly. They think that if they set the treadmill to the same pace they would be running on the road that they are training at that pace. That is just not true. You need to set a treadmill at a 1.5% incline just to simulate the equivalent effort of running on perfectly flat ground. Running on the road has hills, uneven surfaces, varying wind and other conditions that you do not get on a treadmill. So, while a treadmill can be helpful, only use it as a very rare substitute for running outside on the road.

As I talked about in the previous chapter, you might need to change our training schedule around if the weather is bad. Instead of just skipping a workout day altogether, cross-training is a great way to stay on schedule and maintain the momentum of your training, which is all part of the mental conditioning.

Cross-training is also a great way to stay in shape and try to stay on your training schedule if you suffer an injury. If you twist an ankle or develop shin splints or some other kind of injury, do not just drop out of training completely. Use cross-training and other low-impact leg exercises to maintain conditioning while you recover.

To leave comments or questions about this chapter on the website, go to this chapter on:
www.YouCanGoTheDistance.com/book

Yasso 800s: Speed + Endurance

I believe God made me for a purpose, but He also made me fast, and when I run I feel His pleasure.

— Eric Liddell

There is really only one way to learn how to run fast and that is: *Run fast!*

When I first started running marathons, I dreaded the speed workouts that were part of the various training programs I tried. Not only did I not enjoy the workouts themselves, they were also just too complicated—too many combinations of distances, intervals, speeds, target heart rates, VO2Max calculations, etc. Those are all great if you are really into the science of running. Me? I am just an ordinary guy who loves to run and wants to run faster, but who also wants to keep it simple!

So guess what? I usually skipped the speed workouts and just focused on the mid-distance and long runs.

Because I skipped the speed workouts, however, I never could run as fast as I wanted to run.

I do not remember if it was from a friend or from an article I read about running, but somehow, several years ago, I discovered the "Yasso 800," a speed workout invented by well-known runner, coach, and Runner's World author, Bart Yasso.

As soon as I heard about Yasso 800s, I knew I had to try them. As soon as I tried them, I was hooked!

Let me explain Yasso 800s to you so you can try them and see if they work for you.

First, let's break down the name: "Yasso" is from the inventor's last name, Bart Yasso. "800" is for 800 meters. Hence the name, "Yasso 800s." With me so far? Good!

What Bart discovered for himself and then started teaching to other marathon runners is that, if you can build up to doing 10 repetitions of 800 meters (.5 mi, or 2 laps around a track) at a target pace, you should be able to run your marathon at your target time.

The formula could not be easier! You simply take your Marathon Goal time in hours/minutes and convert that time to minutes/seconds. You use that as the time for running your 800 meter repetitions.

Let me give you are real example. My marathon goal is 3 hours and 30 minutes. Instead of using hours and minutes, just use minutes and seconds. This means I need to run my 800 meters in 3 minutes and 30 seconds. According to Bart's research and real-life experience, if I can build up to doing 10 of those repetitions in a single workout, I should be able to run a marathon at my desired 3 hours and 30 minutes. (Of course, you still need to do the rest of your mid-distance and long runs!)

Here is how it actually breaks down during the workout: I do a 1 mile warm-up jog to the track near my house. Because my marathon goal is 3 hours and 30 minutes, my target 800 meter target time is 3 minutes and 30 seconds, which equates to a 7 minute per mile pace. I start running my 800, looking at my GPS watch occasionally to check my pace and adjust accordingly. After completing the 800, I do a very easy—walking/jogging—recovery lap. Then I repeat this process for however many reps I need to do for that workout. When I am done, I do an easy 1 mile recovery jog back home.

So here is another example at a different pace. Let us suppose you want to run your first marathon in 5 hours. That means you would do your Yasso 800s in

5 minutes (which just happens to be a 10 minute per mile pace).

For beginners, I recommend starting with 2 Yasso 800s for your first workout. If you are able to do both 800s at the target pace, then try to add 1 more every other week throughout your training schedule. You will discover later in the schedule that it is hard to add those extra reps! When the rep count gets higher, in Bart's own words, this is a "brutal workout"! Do not get frustrated; just keep trying to add reps until you get to the magic number 10!

Here is an important tip that I constantly have to re-mind myself. I always like to do better than my goals, so I have a tendency to run the 800s faster than I should. When the rep count gets high, it is extremely hard to get in those last reps at the target pace and I usually feel frustrated because the last few come in slower than target.

Do not run faster than you need to, especially at the beginning! This is crucial for your mental condition-ing, too, because it is so tempting to go out faster than you should during your marathon. You will re-gret it if you do. Save your energy for the last few reps. Teach your brain to trust the training plan and training paces. Getting ahead of the plan usually causes more harm than it does good.

When looking at your training schedule, you will want to try to get to 10 Yasso 800s around 3 to 4 weeks before your marathon. Do not try to do 10 of these with only 1 to 2 weeks before your race because you will need those two weeks to taper (recover)— which I talk about in a later chapter.

No access to a track? You can do this just as easily on the road if you are able to measure out a 1/2 mile stretch. Run out and back, nice and easy, as a warm-up. Then run out at your Yasso 800s pace and simply jog back to the starting point. I sometimes do this just to break up the monotony of doing the same workout week after week on the track.

The reason Yasso 800s is such a great workout is twofold: First, because you are running much faster than your target marathon pace, you are teaching your body how to run fast. Second, 800 meters is a long enough distance that your body is learning how to hold a faster pace over a longer distance, thus building endurance! You will need both speed and endurance to reach your marathon goal on race day!

Yasso 800s have definitely helped me become a faster, stronger marathon runner. I believe they will help you too! Give them a try and let me know how it goes.

For more information on Yasso 800s, you should visit Bart online:

Website: **www.bartyasso.com**

Twitter: **www.twitter.com/BartYasso**

Facebook: **www.facebook.com/Yasso800s**

Yasso 800s is one of the core workouts in the YCGTD Marathon Training Plan. For more details on the plan and how to do Yasso 800s, go here: **www.YouCanGoTheDistance.com/plan**

To leave comments or questions about this chapter on the website, go to this chapter on:
www.YouCanGoTheDistance.com/book

Tempo Runs

Train like Kenyans: Tempo, Tempo, Tempo!

Many elite athletes, especially Kenyan runners, believe that the Tempo Run is the single most important workout you can do to get faster at any distance. I've found this to be true in my own training.

Tempo Runs, combined with Yasso 800s have dramatically improved my speed.

But what in the world is a "Tempo Run"?

If you do a Google search for "tempo runs," you will find that they are also called Threshold or Lactate-Threshold or LT runs. You will also find many detailed explanations about oxygen metabolism and hydrogen ions and fatigue points; all of which make for interesting (yawn) science and theory, but I just want to run!

By now you should know that I like to keep things simple. I simplified my speed workouts by just doing Yasso 800s. There are many complicated formulas for how to do perfect Tempo Runs, but, once again, I have simplified them to meet my needs.

This is what a Tempo Run workout looks like for me: 1 mile easy warm-up, then 5 to 10 miles at Tempo pace, then a 1 mile cool-down jog.

I base all of my training paces on the Marathon Goal and its corresponding Race Pace (RP). The Yasso 800s are based on Marathon Goal, but Tempo Runs and Long Runs are based on the target Race Pace. Many programs will have you use previous 5K or 10K results to determine Tempo pace, but using RP works best for me.

Tempo Run pace should be 30 to 40 seconds per mile faster than RP. For example, my Race Pace (RP) is 8:00 per mile, so my Tempo pace is around 7:30 per mile (7:20 for shorter tempo runs). If your RP is 10:00 per mile, your Tempo pace would be 9:30 per mile. (If you need help determining your RP, see the chapter: First Things First: Set A Goal)

For beginners, start with 2 miles at your Tempo pace and add to it throughout your schedule. Try to build up to 10 miles at Tempo pace near the end of your training schedule.

If you are using the YCGTD Marathon Training Plan, you will see a specific weekly schedule of how far and how fast to run. For example, in Week 12, the Tempo Run is "7 mi @ RP – 30". This means that you will run 7 miles at a pace that is 30 seconds faster than your Race Pace (RP – 30). Assumed in this is a 1 mile warm-up and a 1-mile cool-down, for a total of 9 miles that day.

The goal of the Tempo run is to get you used to running longer distances at a pace that is slightly faster than you will run during your marathon. Not only will this build the strength and endurance you'll need for the marathon, it also has the added benefit of making your RP seem easier come race day. In other words, once you get used to running at 7:30 per mile, it seems slow to run at 8:00 per mile, and that's the goal of the Tempo Run.

Tempo Runs will help you develop your running rhythm or "Tempo", stride, and breathing. Getting in a Tempo Runs each week will definitely help you improve your speed and endurance.

So get out there and pound some pavement! You've got a marathon to train for. Get at it!

To leave comments or questions about this chapter on the website, go to this chapter on:
www.YouCanGoTheDistance.com/book

The Long Run: You CAN Go the Distance!

*Who can go the distance? We'll find out in the long run...
Who is gonna make it? We'll find out in the long run.*
— *"The Long Run"* by The Eagles

If you want to be a marathon runner, there is no way around this one: You've got to put in the miles. Specifically, you've got to do your Long Runs! Period.

Speed work will definitely make you faster. Tempo Runs will also make you faster and build endurance while helping you find your race-pace "tempo." But the backbone workout of the marathon runner is the Long Run.

Let me be straight with you right up front. Long Runs are what keep most people from ever even attempting a marathon. They look at a training plan and see 12, 15, 18 & 20 mile runs in the schedule and say to themselves: "I barely even finished a 10K (6.2 miles); there's no way I could run 15, let alone 20 or 26.2 miles!"

You might be thinking this very same thought. Let me tell you this: you are wrong! YOU CAN DO IT!

The hardest part of running a marathon is the decision to do it! Believing that you can run the distance and then actually stepping out your front door to try it is much more than 50% of the effort!

I believe, more than any other sport, the marathon requires not only great physical endurance, but great mental endurance as well. If you believe you can do it, and you train your body and your brain properly, you will run a marathon!

Here is how to do your Long Runs:

The most important thing to do on your Long Runs is slow down! That's right, slow way down!

You have been doing Yasso 800s and Tempo runs, so your body is getting used to running fast. Now you need to do just the opposite and run slowly! And that can be harder than it sounds!

Your Long Runs should be run somewhere between 60 to 90 seconds per mile slower than your Race Pace (RP). If you are an intermediate or advanced runner, you can go 45 to 60 seconds slower, but never less than 45 seconds!

So let me do the heavy math for you with a real example. My RP is 8:00 per mile, so I will be doing my

Long Runs somewhere between a 9:00 to 9:30 per mile pace. If your RP is 10:00 per mile, your Long Runs should be between 11:00 to 11:30 per mile.

I know what you are thinking: "How can I possibly run my marathon at Race Pace if I never do my long training runs at or faster than Race Pace?" Trust me. It just works!

In my early days, I did not believe this theory either and I did my Long Runs much faster than I should have. In most cases, I got injured or was too sore to do the next week's workouts and I actually lost training ground instead of gaining. So please take my advice and do your Long Runs slowly.

If you are intimidated by the distance and are worried that you might not be able to complete a 20-mile run even at 90 seconds per mile slower than RP, that is OK. If you are a beginner, I do not want you to focus on time at all during your Long Runs. Focus on the distance, not the pace.

What you are really trying to accomplish on these runs is to get your feet, legs and brain used to being out on the road for a long time. By running your 20-mile Long Runs around 90 seconds slower than Race

Pace, you will be spending almost as much time on the road as you will come race day going the full 26.2.

You should be running at a pace that is slow enough to have a conversation with a running buddy. If you can talk about work, kids, hobbies, etc, throughout the entire long run, you are doing it right. If all you can do is give simple one or two word answers to questions because you are out of breath, you are running too fast!

At the end of your Long Run, you should be tired, but not totally exhausted! Save "exhausted" for race day!

Go the distance!

Another thing you absolutely must do on your Long Runs is this: Go the entire distance! Do not cut them short!

This is another mistake I have made: If I am having a bad day and struggling to maintain my pace within the 60-90 second window—meaning I'm going even slower than that—I have often just given up and cut the run short. This is a big mistake. On Long Runs, distance is much more important than speed—walking the distance is better than cutting it short!

I want you to go the entire distance even at the expense of time. This is especially true of the 20-mile Long Runs! If you need to walk the last 5 or more miles, I don't care. Just go the distance! Going the distance teaches your body to exert physical effort over a long period of time, and, I think most importantly, it trains your brain to not give up!

Getting your Long Runs in will make you feel great about yourself and will bolster your confidence about finishing the big 26.2. Cutting them short will leave you feeling uncertain about your progress and will cause you to question your ability to complete the marathon. Set yourself up for success. Go the entire distance!

I also recommend, regardless of what your particular training program says, that you get in at least two 20-mile Long Runs. Some plans only have you do a single 20-miler and I do not think that gives you enough physical or mental long-distance training. Two or more is best, in my opinion. My YCGTD Marathon Training Plan includes four 20-mile runs.

2 Tips to ensure you finish your long run

Tip 1: I am a big fan of coach Jeff Galloway's RUN-WALK-RUN™ method for training and racing. The concept is amazingly simple: Run some, then walk some, then run some more! His research and testing with thousands of runners proves this method can help you go farther, faster.

You can learn more about this method on Jeff's website at: **www.jeffgalloway.com**

During my Long Runs, I actually walk for about 30 seconds every 2 miles. This gives me a chance to relax and drink. I chose 2-mile intervals because that is the interval of water stations in most marathons. It is actually quite practical to walk through the water stations since it is very difficult to run and drink from a cup!

Not only does walking every 2 miles help with my stamina, there is also a huge mental benefit. Remember that a marathon is as much a mental race as it is physical. Many runners drop out near the end of the race because their brains have convinced them they could not go another 5 miles, when, physically, they could have. (See my story in The Finish Line chapter as an example of this.)

This method allows me to mentally break the marathon into 13 segments. Instead of thinking about running 26 miles, I only have to think about running

2 miles 13 times. For a 20-mile training run, I only have to run 2 miles 10 times! Breaking long, daunting tasks into manageable segments is a great way to ensure success! It helps me, so maybe it will help you.

If you're just starting out, this method will really help you. It is OK to walk every mile! You may even want to do it based on time. Run for 5 minutes, walk for 1. Do not be ashamed to walk. Many elite marathoners use this method!

Tip 2: Set yourself up for success, not for failure! Do not do your Long Runs on a loop course. Do an out-and-back course. Why? You cannot cheat on an out-and-back. It is just as far back as it was out!

You might not be as prone to temptation as I am, but I know myself. If I get really tired and there is a shorter way home, I am usually going to take short-cut!

The out-and-back course also helps me mentally. There is a clear 1/2 way point and it always seems easier heading back home than it does going out. I am always highly motivated to get back home and put my feet up!

Remember what I said at the beginning? The most important thing about your long run is going the full distance that your program calls for, even if you have to walk some (or a lot) of it. Do not worry about how long it takes you. You are teaching your body and your brain to go the distance and you will be glad you did come race day!

Another reason I like out-and-back courses is they are easy to map out and they are reusable for all of your long run distances. If you do not have a GPS watch, use a mapping website like **www.MapMyRun.com**, or, easiest yet, simply get in your car and drive 10 miles watching the odometer and noting the landmarks at the miles! The same course you use for your 20-mile runs also work for 18, 16, 14, etc.

Course Planning Tip: Try to plan out your Long Run course so that it has roughly the same amount of hills as your planned marathon course. It doesn't help to have a really flat training course if you are training for a hilly marathon!

So put on your headphones and listen to The Eagles as you run. "Who can go the distance?" YOU CAN!!

To leave comments or questions about this chapter on the website, go to this chapter on:

www.YouCanGoTheDistance.com/book

Long Run Recovery

This chapter is all about recovering from your Long Runs!

Did you get in a Long Run of 12 or more miles?

Did you run it slowly like I recommended? I hope so!

Here is a section of a blog post I did about one of my 20-mile Long Runs:

"I think there must be something psychological that happens with me and my 20-mile runs. 3 weeks ago I ran 18 miles and had no trouble going the distance at exactly the pace I had planned. What is it with those extra 2 miles? I don't know... I've been saying that the marathon is just as much a mental race as it is physical... Anyway, I got it in—albeit slower than planned— and I feel a big sense of accomplishment. Now it's time to recover!"

Why do I need a recovery period?

While I am no doctor of sports medicine, I have learned the basics of how muscles develop strength. You probably have, too, but it does not hurt to review and think about it in a metaphor.

We do not build strength while running. We build strength while resting!

You do not build strength while you are actually doing a strenuous activity like running or weight lifting. Those activities, while you are doing them, stress and tear down muscle tissue. It is during the rest/recovery period that your body rebuilds the muscles and makes them stronger.

Think of it this way: Let's say our muscles are like levees that keep a river from flooding the town. When the flood comes, torrents of water stress the levees and start to break them down. Engineers know that it is pretty useless to try to rebuild or repair the levees while it is flooding. However, when the flood waters recede, they inspect the damage and make repairs in such a way that the levee will be better and stronger in those weakened places and ready for the strain the next time a flood comes.

Our bodies handle stresses in much the same way. When we are out doing our Long Runs, or speed and tempo workouts, we are bringing a flood of stress to those muscles. Our body tries to meet the requirements as best it can at the time but the process of exercising actually strains and tears the muscle fibers making them weaker. However, while we rest, the body is busy at work repairing the muscles, making them stronger in anticipation of you doing the same thing, or worse, the next time you run.

If you fail to give your body enough time to make the necessary repairs, the muscles will continue to weaken and you will suffer an over-use injury and jeopardize your entire training plan.

You can recognize an over-use injury like this: your training has been going great, you are running strong and feeling like you are ahead of your training goals. Then, out of nowhere, you blow out a knee, or twist an ankle, or get a sharp pain in your hip that just won't go away. Over-use injuries are from not allowing the muscles that support those joints to have enough time to recover and rebuild, so they weaken and your joints pay the penalty!

Do your body a huge favor. Give it the rest it needs. It will reward you with strength!

I know many marathon training programs have you running 4, 5 or even 6 days a week. Personally, I think this is too much. I actually only run 3 days a week! I know my body and I know I need the break between workouts. I run on Tuesday, Thursday and

Saturday. I cross-train or just rest on my non-running days.

I will add, however, that it may be OK for you to be running 5 or 6 days a week as long as a few of them are just leisurely jogs, not intense training runs. And I'm OK with what are called "recovery jogs" as long as they are exactly that: slow, short jogs simply for the purpose of loosening up and working out the stiffness.

How do I rest after a long run? Well, that's easy enough. I just rest! I get off my feet as soon as possible. While I still have to function and interact with my family, I try not to do anything rigorous for a few hours after my run.

I normally take 2 days off after a long run. I usually do my long runs on Saturday mornings, so I don't run again until Tuesday morning. By that time, I am usually recovered and ready to start another training week.

What do I eat and drink for long run recovery?

This is another question I get frequently. Again, I'm no nutritionist or even a health-food nut, so many of you will already have your own favorites. But here is the basics of what I do and what many other coaches and training programs recommend:

Not only do your muscles need the rest in order to rebuild, they need the proper supplies—just like re-building a levee! You need to give your body lots of fluid and lots of nutrients!

The most important thing to do after a hard workout, especially a Long Run, is drink!

Even though you were (or you should have been) drinking during your Long Run, your body needs as much fluid as possible to wash away the acids and waste that accumulated in your sore muscles.

Protein is also very important for recovery. I like to eat cottage cheese or plain Greek yogurt with fresh blueberries or sliced apples after a Long Run. I also like to drink chocolate instant breakfast mix in 2% milk.

I also love fruit smoothies as a recovery drink!

For a much more complete review of nutrition for Long Run recovery, see the chapter "Nutrition: Choose the Right Fuels!"

So, you've done your Long Run! Now, give yourself
the reward of ample time to rest!

To leave comments or questions about this chapter
on the website, go to this chapter on:
www.YouCanGoTheDistance.com/book

Develop a Race-Day Routine, Now!

I want you to start thinking about race day! Today!

Start developing your race-day routine, now!

You are thinking: "What? The race is still many weeks away. Why should I start thinking about a race-day routine now?"

Let me stress that it is never too soon to start practicing what you will do before and during the race!

Many first-time marathoners spend so much time training their bodies to go the distance that their bodies are ready to run the race, but they do not have a race-day plan. They have not thought through what to do the night before, what to have for breakfast, how frequently they will stop at the water stops, whether or not they will run with their own water bottle or use the water provided along the course, or how to deal with the many issues that can arise during the race. Get the point?

Now is the time to start thinking about these things and actually start practicing them. It is time to think of every Long Run you do as a practice of marathon day!

Do not wait until the week before to come up with some plan that you have never actually practiced!

It is important that race day be as close, in every way, to every other long training run as possible. You will have enough pre-race jitters to deal with, so you do not want to have to adjust to situations you have never practiced for on top of that!

Trust me on this! Your race will go much smoother if you've got a race-day routine.

Let me give you some suggestions of things to practice and to start thinking about:

What time of day do you do your long training runs? I realize it is hard for many of you to do your training runs in the mornings, but let me specifically stress the importance of doing your Long Runs in the mornings and doing them on the same day as your planned marathon.

Almost every marathon is held early on a Saturday or Sunday morning. If you are practicing your Long Runs on a different day of the week or different time than your planned race, you are not practicing for your race. When race day comes, it will not be your normal routine to get up early for a long run on that morning. You will have to do things you have not practiced.

Here is another scenario: what do you do if you wake up on the morning of your long training runs and it is raining? Do you just roll over and go back to sleep? Do you get up and cross-train instead? If the answer to either of these is "yes", is that what you are going to do on race morning? NO, of course not!

If it is raining on race day, you will go run in the rain, but it will be a condition you have not trained for so you have no idea how you will perform. I wrote in a previous chapter about the importance of training in all conditions. Here is where it really applies. Get up, go out, and practice running in the rain!

Practice what you will eat and drink before and during the race. What to eat and drink is probably the most important race-day routine to develop!

If you are going to run a marathon on a Saturday morning, experiment with different foods for dinner on Friday nights so you can see how they make you feel the next morning during your Long Run.

I know many races sponsor a big pasta dinner the night before the race and many runners and coaches have talked about the importance of "carb-loading" the night before. That does not work well for me. I usually carb-load on Wednesday night and then have a light, bland meal of chicken and potatoes on Friday night. Experiment with different diets the night before your Long Runs to see what works best for you.

When you find a meal that sits really well with you and gives you the necessary fuel to get you through your Long Runs, stick with it. Most importantly, do not change anything about that diet the night before your race!

Now, what about in the morning? Start experimenting with whether or not to eat breakfast, have coffee or juice, etc. before your Long Runs. It is better to learn early in your training if something is going to make you vomit or give you diarrhea 15 miles later! I have learned this for myself the hard way! Find what works for you now, rather than doing something new on race morning only to find out you made a bad choice.

How about during the run? What are you going to drink? Water, Gatorade, Powerade, or some other drink? If you are going to run with a hydration belt, experiment with different fluids. If you are planning to race without a hydration belt because of the weight, decide now whether you are going to drink the provided water or sports drink—almost all marathons provide both on the course. Find out well ahead of time what your race will offer and start training with that. If they are going to serve Powerade along the course, it doesn't do you any good to train with Gatorade!

Many runners use other fuel sources like energy gels or power bars. Try different ones. Many races will hand out these gels, energy bars, and fruits, like bananas and oranges, along the course. Take my advice, if you have not trained with any of these, do not take them during the race, no matter how tempting they look! If you have no idea how your stomach will react to a banana 20 miles into a race, you do not want to learn that on race day! The time to learn is now. Take some of these with you on your Long Runs to see how they work for you.

Band-Aids and BodyGlide

Now is also the best time to practice protecting your body!

Band-Aids and BodyGlide are my best friends on a long run!

I have one toe, my "pinky" toe on my left foot, that tends to blister on Long Runs. I have tried many things to prevent it, but I have learned a simple Band-Aid on that toe does the trick!

However, the most import place I use Band-Aids may come as a surprise! Most ladies I have talked to do not have this problem because of their snug-fitting sports bras, but almost all men I have talked to have a problem with nipple chaffing!

I have not had it this bad before, but a friend of mine crossed the finish line of a marathon with two big, bright red blood stains on his shirt. His nipples had chaffed so badly they were bleeding. That's painful! One Band-Aid on each nipple makes for a much more enjoyable run for me! Try it, men!

Still talking about chaffing, I very often experience chaffing between my inner thighs and butt crack! I have tried lots of remedies, but a bar of BodyGlide solves the problem for me. I usually carry a small bar in my running belt just in case I need to reapply mid-run.

So I have given you a bunch of stuff to start thinking about and practicing. I really want you to develop a mind-set where you think of every long training run as a practice race. Not practicing the speed of the race, of course, but practicing the mechanics and the routines you will go through in preparation for and during the race. You may find it helpful to keep a check-list of the things you've tried so you can remember to do those things every time.

If you develop your race-day routine now, it will pay big dividends for you on race day!

To leave comments or questions about this chapter on the website, go to this chapter on:
www.YouCanGoTheDistance.com/book

Roll with the Changes!

A marathon training program is usually between 16 to 20 weeks long. Inevitably, changes and challenges will come up during those weeks, so I want to talk about how to handle them as race day approaches.

I know I wrote about how you need to train in all conditions—and that is true—however, life happens and situations change. Running should not be stressful and your training plan is not etched in stone. Keep it high in priority, but be flexible with your training schedule.

You've got to learn to roll with the changes!

"Keep on rollin'! Keep on rollin'! Oh, you've got to learn to roll with the changes" — REO Speedwagon

When I started my current training schedule it was early Summer. However, Summer blew by and early Autumn was here before I knew it.

Autumn in Virginia is always a time for changes. The kids are back in school; my work schedule is shifting back into a more normal routine; the weather is cooling off and we are getting more rain; and the days are getting shorter, so I am running in the dark more. Lots of changes.

It is our human nature to resist change, but, in order to succeed, we have to adapt as changes come our way.

A big danger we all face as runners is letting these seasonal changes derail our training.

If you ran early in the mornings during the Summer because it was cooler, the kids were still asleep and the sun was just coming up. It is natural to struggle to maintain that schedule come Fall. Now you are up early getting the kids ready for school and it is dark outside. Your normal routine has been disrupted by seasonal and situational changes.

How do you handle these changes? You have to adapt, adjust and roll with it. But do not quit! Change your routine.

Trust in the fact that I am preaching to myself here, too, because I am not immune to these changes and the disruptions to my routine. There are often crazy weeks full of crazy temperature changes, rain and schedule conflicts for my family and, as a result, I do not always get in my mid-week Tempo Runs... such is life. The training schedule is important, but you should never become a slave to it.

Here are just a few simple (and probably obvious) things you can do to adapt to the changes:

Mentally prepare and accept that changes can and will come. Marathons are a mind game and if you emotionally prepare yourself to embrace changes, and even welcome them, your training will still be successful. Shift your marathon training schedule to meet your new life schedule. My work schedule allows me to run after I get the kids off to school instead of before. I prefer to run early in the morning, but this modification works for me. If your schedule allows, you can switch to doing a workout during your lunch hour. Believe it or not, this can actually give you a big burst of endorphins that will make you more productive throughout the rest of the afternoon. Find a way to make it work for you without stressing yourself or your family.

Aside from the schedule changes, plan for the seasonal changes to temperature and light conditions.

Start using a headlamp or flashlight if you are running in the dark. Start dressing for cooler temperatures.

I think you get the points I'm trying to make so I will not belabor the issue.

The biggest point I want to make is this: adapting to changes is necessary. The more you prepare for and accept what comes your way, physically and mentally, the more prepared you will be for your race and for your life!

To leave comments or questions about this chapter on the website, go to this chapter on:
www.YouCanGoTheDistance.com/book

Time for a Progress Check

During a marathon, most runners do some self-evaluation and progress checking at the half-marathon, 13.1 miles, mark. We ask ourselves: How am I feeling? Am I ahead of or behind my planned pace? Any unusual aches or pains? Based on how I feel and knowing the weather conditions, do I need to make any mid-course adjustments?

Just as you will inevitably go through this thought process during the race, it is essential you go through it at the mid-point of your training.

How are you doing? Are you getting in your speed and Tempo Runs? Are you getting faster, stronger? How about the Long Runs? Any nagging pains, injuries or other physical or mental concerns?

These are the questions you need to be asking yourself now. And not just asking... realistically answering them is crucial to the rest of your training!

Based on your answers to the questions above, you may be doing great and are right on schedule or you may need to make some adjustments to your physical and emotional expectations.

Please, if this is going to be your first marathon, do not under estimate the amount of emotional endurance this race requires and the impact it will have on you if train hard and do not meet your goal. If you need to make some adjustments to your race goals, that is OK! It is better to make them now, by choice, instead of 1 or 2 weeks before the race, or, worse yet, during the race, out of necessity!

It's time for a Benchmark Run!

One of the best ways to determine if your training really is on track is to do a "benchmark run."

A benchmark run can be a few different things. It can be a shorter-distance race like a half marathon or a 10K. Or it can be a run you do on your own or with a friend at a specific pace.

"How do I determine the pace for my benchmark run?" you ask. I knew you were going to ask, so here is how I do it:

Back in the chapter on goal setting, I recommended using Greg McMillan's Running Calculator, also known as an "equivalent effort" calculator, to help you determine your ideal marathon goal.

Here is the link to the calculator:

www.YouCanGoTheDistance.com/calculator

The concept is very simple. Plug in your best race time for any given distance and it will tell you what time/pace you should be able to perform for other distances. For example, if your best 10K is 50 minutes, you should, with proper training, be able to run a marathon in 3:54 (3 hours, 54 minutes).

To determine the pace for a benchmark run, just use the calculator backwards. If your goal is to complete a marathon in 4 hours, you should be able to race a 10K in 51:09 (an 8:14 pace) or a 5K in 24:38 (a 7:56 pace). Plug your marathon goal into the calculator to get your specific 10K and 5K paces.

Now, do not misunderstand me. These equivalent effort paces assume that you are in peak condition to run your 4 hour marathon. You are not yet! So do not go race a 10K this weekend and expect to finish in 51:09! In fact, trying to do so can cause an injury or make you too sore to continue with next week's training!

Somewhere around 10 weeks into your training, I want you to do a 5K benchmark run using the pace suggested by the calculator for a 10K. In other words, try to run a 5K as close as possible to your target 10K pace. Using the example above, you should try to run your 5K at a 8:14 pace.

I recommend you swap out one of your Yasso 800s or Tempo Run workout days and make that a 5K benchmark race day.

If you can run a 5K at your target 10K pace at 10 weeks into your marathon training, you are right on target!

If you come close but fall a little short of the 10K target pace, do not worry about it. Just keep training.

However, if you really pushed with everything you had for your benchmark 5K and were significantly off of the 10K target pace, that's OK. You are NOT a failure! You just need to adjust your goal to something more realistic. Go ahead and plug the time for the 5K you just ran into the calculator, do a mental reset of your expectations, and use the new marathon estimate as your new marathon goal! Remember, the most important thing is to set yourself up for success and this is a great way to do that!

Under-trained is better than Over-trained!

I am willing to bet many of you reading this are just like me. If I think I am falling a bit behind in my training, I will push really hard to catch up! Do you, too? I thought so. Do not do it!

I want you to resist the urge to train harder if you are falling a bit behind schedule. I have done it before and I have a friend who seems to do it every single time. We push harder in the last few weeks and, sure enough, we get injured!

If you are using a well-known, time tested training program, stay on it. Trust the experience that went into developing the plan!

I would much rather go into a marathon a little bit under-trained than to push too hard, over-train, and get injured or not perform well because you were just worn out come race day.

To leave comments or questions about this chapter on the website, go to this chapter on:
www.YouCanGoTheDistance.com/book

Rock Lobster Running

This chapter, it is all about music and rhythm!

Can "Rock Lobster" Improve Your Running?

I like to listen to music when I run. Most of my friends who run do too!

Listening to music while you run can certainly improve your running experience.

Many runners like to talk about and compare their running play lists. What do you listen to? Classic Rock, Country, Pop, Hip-Hop, Jazz? Do you crank it up loud or just keep it soft in the background? There are as many personal preferences as there are runners!

There is, however, a very important factor that most runners do not talk about or even take into consideration when putting together a play list. And it is a factor that can dramatically affect your marathon training!

Tempo, tempo, tempo! No, I am not talking about Tempo Runs that I wrote about in a previous chapter. I am talking about the tempo of your music.

Most runners just pick a bunch of songs they really like or that keep them pumped up. They do not think about the fact that they will naturally adjust their running stride to the tempo—some call it "cadence"—of the music they are listening to and are, therefore, constantly changing their running rhythm with every song.

I do not remember where I first learned about the ideal running tempo, but I know my running style has radically changed for the better now that I have put it into practice for the last two years.

"Rock Lobster" by the B-52s is one of the perfect running songs! Why? It's exactly 180 BPM (beats per minute) — the ideal running tempo!

Someone studied elite runners for multiple distances and they all, regardless of height, weight, gender or nationality had one thing in common. They all ran at a tempo of about 180 beats (or steps) per minute. Most of the runners studied actually had no idea that this was their stride-rate. It was just how they ran. This study has become very popular and many of the new elite athletes have been trained to run at this pace.

Running at 180 steps per minute (or 3 steps per second!) will improve the way you run by forcing you to shorten your stride.

As far as stride length is concerned, shorter and faster is better than longer and slower!

Also, as for tempo, consistency is king! You should try to run at the same stride rate all the time! Increase or decrease your speed by lengthening or shortening your stride, but keep your feet moving at the same tempo. This is also true for running up hills or down hills.

If you are not already doing it, I want you to try it. It is going to feel awkward at first. But if you keep at it, it will be fun, and it will become your normal running rhythm and your running will improve!

180 BPM – The How To:

The easiest way to start running at 180 beats (steps) per minute is to practice jogging in place. Look at your watch and count to 3 for each second. So count 1 2 3, 1 2 3, 1 2 3, so that the 1s fall on each second. Start jogging in place to that tempo. Once you've got the rhythm down, keep counting to yourself and start moving forward so you are actually jogging. Keep your strides really short to start. Go slowly and gradually increase the length of your stride until you are running!

Many of us have iPhones or Androids or some other smart phones. One thing you can do is download a metronome app and set it to 180 BPM and run to the clicks of the metronome.

But this chapter was supposed to be about music! OK, let's find the right songs and take our music to the streets!

I found a great product called MixMeister BPM Analyzer. It is FREE and available for both PC and Mac!

Here's the link to download:
www.YouCanGoTheDistance.com/bpmanalyzer

It will analyze all of the songs (MP3s) in your music library and update each of your songs with its BPM so your music software (I use iTunes) will automatically know the BPM each song. In iTunes, it is really easy to sort songs by BPM and simply drag the songs that are right at 90/180 BPM into a playlist.

Notice that I said 90/180 BPM. 90 BPM is the same tempo as 180 BPM, so do not let that confuse you.

Now you can really analyze the music that you've been listening to and know if it is the right tempo for you.

It was not until I really started to apply this technique of picking songs and being very intentional about my running tempo that I realized just how inconsistent my running tempo had been. I had music in my play list that was as slow as 75/150 BPM. In order to maintain my speed, I was having to really increase my stride length to maintain tempo with my music. Then the next song might be really fast, and I would have to change again…

Now that all of my songs are very close to the same tempo, my running tempo and stride length is much more consistent and my legs and knees are much happier about that!

Like trying anything new, this will certainly feel strange at first. It took me several weeks before I was running at a consistent 180 BPM without thinking about it. Now, I know my play list songs by heart so I can just sing them in my head even if I am running unplugged.

So go ahead and try this and let me know how it works out for you!

Also, it would be great if you posted the names of some of your favorite playlist songs in the comments!

Now, you've got a marathon to train for. So get your 180 BPM groove on and get rockin'!

To leave comments or questions about this chapter on the website, go to this chapter on:
www.YouCanGoTheDistance.com/book

Is it Time for New Shoes?

So let's talk about shoes!

When you are about a month away from your marathon, you should seriously evaluate whether or not you need new shoes. You need several weeks to break them in and allow your feet and legs to get used to them.

Do not run a marathon in a new pair of shoes!

In fact, do not run a marathon in *anything* new. Be sure you have done at least one long run in exactly what you are going to wear on race day. Race day is not the time to discover something does not fit right or rubs you in a bad way.

So how do you know when it is time to buy new running shoes?

I am certainly no expert on shoes, so I decided to call my go-to guy for all things related to running gear so I could give you the best advice.

Jeff Van Horn—no relation to me—is the owner of Luck Foot, an amazing running store in the Richmond, Virginia area. Jeff has a degree in Sports

Medicine and is an expert on human bio-mechanics, gait analysis, and knows more about shoes and running gear than anyone I know.

Needless to say, Jeff is qualified to answer the question: "When should I get new shoes?"

His first answer to the question is actually the most obvious. You should get new shoes when your current shoes start to get uncomfortable or are no longer doing their job of supporting your feet properly.

Supporting and protecting your feet is, after all, the primary purpose of a shoe. When they are no longer doing that job properly, it is time for a new pair.

The average runner will get roughly 400 miles out of a good pair of running shoes. That number will vary depending on your weight, running style, and where you run—roads, trails, treadmill, etc.

Some things to look at are these:

Tread (Outer-sole): if the tread is wearing through in spots so the mid-sole (cushion) is showing or if the tread is wearing so they no longer can grip the road in slippery or wet conditions, it is time to change.

Mid-sole (cushion): this is the foam or air pockets between the tread and the In-sole. If it has lost its ability to absorb the shocks of running or is starting to crack or separate from the Outer-sole, it is time to change.

Uppers: This is the fabric, the pretty part of the shoe that holds your foot. If it is wearing through in places, particularly around the toes, it is time to change. Also, the upper shoe fabric can stretch, so if your laces are getting longer because you need to tie them tighter to make the shoe fit better, it is time for a change.

Jeff's best advice is this: Go to a local running shoe store and try on an new pair of shoes identical to the ones you are wearing. Jog up and down the aisles. Better yet, if the store will let you, go for a short jog around the parking lot. If you cannot really tell a difference between the new shoes and your current shoes, just keep what you have. If you notice a difference in cushion, fit and stability, then buy the new shoes.

I would also add this to Jeff's advice: if you only have a month before your race and you do need new shoes, buy the very same shoes—brand and model—

that you currently have. Now is not the time to try a completely different brand or style of shoe.

I also highly recommend that you buy your shoes at a locally owned running store rather than a big-name, multi-purpose sports or department store. Not only will you get much better service and advice at a store owned and operated by runners, you will be support-ing your local business and running community. Many of these stores have their own weekly group runs, which is a great way to meet new running friends!

Now, you've got a marathon to train for, so look at your shoes and decide now whether or not you need a new pair! Do not put it off until the week before your race!

Here is a shameless plug for Jeff Van Horn and his Lucky Foot store:

Website: **www.luckyfoot.com**
Facebook: **www.facebook.com/LuckyFootLLC**

To leave comments or questions about this chapter on the website, go to this chapter on:

www.YouCanGoTheDistance.com/book

Proper Running Form

What is the proper running form?

The subject of proper running form is, surprisingly, not a subject that a lot of runners talk about. Most of the runners I have asked say they have never really thought about, nor have they been coached in, the proper way to run.

I have coached many people, including kids on cross-country teams, and I have run a lot of races and seen a lot of different running forms in my life.

Sometimes I will be running behind someone watching them run and I will think to myself "how on earth can he run like that? It looks painful!"

I have also talked to a bunch of former-runners who gave up running because it hurt or never felt comfortable or because they developed knee/hip problems.

Many running related injuries and most of the dissatisfaction with running can be attributed to bad running form.

Where and how your feet land is the most important part of your running form.

Look at the picture above. This guy looks like he is moving along pretty well. It looks like many running strides you have seen before, right?

What is wrong with his form?

His problem is his leg is extended way out in front which will cause his foot to not only strike on the back of his heel, but well in front of his center of gravity.

A lot of runners buy into the dangerous myth that a longer stride is better because you cover more ground with each step. That is absolutely not true! A shorter, faster stride is much more efficient and will dramatically reduce many common running injuries.

Where your feet land is the most important part of running!

When your foot lands in front of your center of gravity it does at least two very bad things:

First, it stops your forward momentum. Your body is jolted to a sudden stop and the weight of your body has to carry you through that jolt in order to roll into the next stride. We want to move forward smoothly without hindering the momentum.

The second bad thing is also the most obvious: it hurts! Because you have just landed on your foot in front of your body, your heel, ankle, shin, knee, hip and lower back all absorb the shock of the landing. This can cause all kinds of injuries and the pain of every stride is often what causes people to stop running.

One of the most common and painful running injuries is shin splints. Shin splints are often caused by landing on your heel in front of your body. As soon as your heel strikes the ground, your shin muscle is jerked violently as it tries to keep your foot from just flopping forward. Many people are able to avoid shin splints simply by adjusting their stride so they land more on the ball of their foot instead of on the heel.

The problem with shoes and what we can learn from the barefoot crowd:

I am not a big fan of barefoot or minimalist running. I am not opposed to it, either. It just isn't my thing right now. However, I think there is a lot we can learn about proper running form by running barefoot!

Do an experiment. Take off your shoes and jog down your street for a few hundred yards and then jog back.

How did it feel? If you actually did it, I bet you immediately changed your running style to avoid landing directly on your heel, didn't you?

Landing on your heel with your leg extended beyond your hips hurts a lot if you are barefoot, but not so much if you are wearing nice, highly cushioned running shoes.

Remember when we were kids and we ran all over the neighborhood barefoot and never thought anything about it? I think we can learn much from watching our kids or other barefoot runners. They naturally adapt to a running form that minimizes the pain of impact. They naturally adopt a proper running form.

The best running form is to have your foot land directly under your hips, directly at your center of gravity.

The goal of each stride is to land and then immediately push off to move your body forward.

If your stride is too far forward, you temporarily stop your forward motion and feel the painful jolt.

If you land too far behind your center of gravity, you feel like you are stumbling forward and do not have an efficient push with each stride.

2 Tips for improving your form:

Start off by simply jogging in place for 15 seconds. Jogging in place naturally maintains your center of gravity. Start moving forward by just leaning your upper body forward a bit. As you start to move, be aware of your center of gravity. As you start running faster, pay attention to where your feet are landing. They should land directly under your hips.

Try running barefoot. Take off your shoes and run slowly for a few minutes. You can even run through your yard or a field. Many people like to start barefoot running on a track. Barefoot running will show you in a dramatic way just how dependent you have become on the padding in your shoes and how that dependency has caused you to develop a bad running form. This will automatically bring you back to the natural running style you were created to have.

When you put your shoes back on, always be thinking about your stride and ask yourself "how would this feel right now if I were barefoot" and adjust your stride accordingly.

Everyone is different and everyone will have a slightly different style of running. That's OK. If I have gotten you to at least think about your running form and to try the experiments I have suggested, then I have accomplished something important. If you have struggled with shin splints or some other nagging knee or hip pain that has not been diagnosed by a doctor as some other condition, at least consider that it could be the result of way you are running. Try to make these changes and see if it helps.

I know for myself that my running has improved and become much more comfortable as I have adapted my stride.

To leave comments or questions about this chapter on the website, go to this chapter on:
www.YouCanGoTheDistance.com/book

Nutrition: Choose the Right Fuels!

I have mentioned in other chapters various nutrition and hydration tips that I have found helpful. However, since I really do want this book to be as helpful and informative as I can make it, I really needed to include a complete chapter on proper nutrition and how important it is to every runner.

The problem with me giving you nutritional advice is that it is just not my area of expertise. The other problem is that most of my friends and family would roll on the floor laughing if they knew I was giving you nutritional advice!

So, to save me from embarrassment, and to get you the best advice possible, I asked fellow runner, Holistic Health Coach, and nutrition expert, Adina Kelman, if she would be willing to write this chapter for me. Adina graciously accepted my request and we are all much better off because of it.

What follows is great advice from someone who, as you will quickly see, knows what she is talking about!

Nutrition: Choose the Right Fuels! By Adina Kelman

Running is my passion and my personal excuse for making my health a priority. It allows me to focus on me, my diet, my sleep, and my overall health. If I eat less nutrient dense foods, my running suffers. If I skimp on sleep too many nights in a row, my following runs are slow and sluggish. If I do not run and I do not create that sacred time which is just for me alone, I am, let's just say, a less than charitable wife and mother. Health and wellness, which includes proper nutrition, can have a profound effect on your running. It is, however, a commitment that begins well before race day. I encourage both new and seasoned runners to educate themselves, independently or with the help of a trained professional, on the benefits of a diet rich in nutrient dense foods. That being said, you have courageously committed to running a marathon and if you have not already done so, it is time to establish some basic, healthy eating habits.

Just like Bruce, I like to keep it simple for myself and my clients. Here are a few **guidelines**:

1. Eat when you are hungry and listen to your body. This sounds simple, but it is advice often overlooked. Estimating calories burned during a run or cross-training workout, whether done by you or your Nike iPod coach, is usually inaccurate as well as ineffective. I personally do not like counting calories or carbs and I try to avoid addition and subtraction in general. I listen to my body, to the demands it makes after a run, and I satisfy those demands with clean, unprocessed foods. Become attuned to your body just as you do when you are running. Pay attention to cravings—your body is telling you what it needs. That doesn't mean that a sweet craving is license to down a couple of donuts just as a hankering for salt doesn't mean you should eat a bag of potato chips. Search for the healthier alternative that will satisfy you. Respect your body and what it is asking for and satisfy your appetite with real food.

2. Eat lots of fresh vegetables and fruits. Loaded with antioxidant vitamins, minerals, and micronutrients, fruits and vegetables should be a large part of a healthy diet. Eat as many vegetables, and to a slightly lesser extent, fruits, as you wish. Aim to include some form of fresh produce at every meal. At breakfast, include berries. If you are having a sandwich for lunch, throw some avocado, sprouts, or sun-dried tomatoes onto it. At dinner, aim to fill half your plate with vegetables. Try to include as many colors as you can. This is an easy way to insure that you are benefiting from all the many vitamins, minerals, and micronutrients found in vegetables.

3. Include some form of protein with each meal.

Every cell in the human body contains protein. It is a major part of the skin, muscles, organs, and glands. Protein is also found in all body fluids, except bile and, in general, urine. The amino acids that make up a protein molecule aid in muscular growth and repair. The current dietary reference intake (DRI) for protein for individuals over 18 years of age, regardless of physical activity, is 0.8 grams per kilogram of body weight per day. Divide your current weight by 2.2 (this converts pounds to kilograms) and multiply by .8 to get the recommended amount of protein. (i.e., a 100 pound person weighs about 45 kilograms. 45 x 0.8 = 36 grams of protein). Guidelines for protein intake increase as you factor your endurance program, strength training, and recovery into your routine. As I said before, I avoid math and formulas when I can. I have never calculated my protein intake and I do not plan to ever include this as part of my daily routine. Instead, aim to eat a serving size approximate to the palm of your hand for your main meals and less if you are having a snack. It is that simple.

4. Enjoy good quality fats. Primarily a form of energy reserves and insulation in the body, fats can be

burned to make energy when we are not getting enough from our diet. Fats are important in transporting nutrients, such as vitamins A, D, E, and K. I rely on good quality olive oil, nuts, seeds, and avocado as my primary source of fat as well as the occasional use of coconut oil. The Academy of Nutrition and Dietetics Position Paper on Nutrition and Athletic Performance recommends athletes get 20 to 35 percent of their total energy intake from fat. This provides enough fat to replenish post training fuel stores while allowing room for adequate carbohydrates and protein consumption. Again, I do not adhere to these percentages, but instead eat what I am in the mood for which varies day to day. If weight is not an issue, I would encourage you to do the same. Becoming attuned to the needs of your body is an invaluable tool that will serve you well as the demands of training fluctuate from day to day.

5. Eat whole grains. This does not mean cereal in a box. There are a variety of grains available to you. Experiment. Try quinoa, millet, amaranth. Choose brown rice over white. Whole grains are complex carbohydrates that provide steady energy and serve as a source of vitamins, minerals, fiber and protein. The recommended dietary allowance for carbohydrates is 130 grams per day. The amount of recommended carbohydrates varies so significantly from one individual to the next and from one dietary theory to the other, that I think the more important focus should be on the quality of the carbohydrate rather than the quantity. The goal is to incorporate, as much as possible, whole grains that have not been stripped, processed, or pulverized into a flour. The more intact the grain, the better.

6. Power up your meals with some super-foods. Establish some basic healthy eating habits before you start powering up. Just as in your training, you need to establish a solid base before you layer longer runs and more intense workouts. The same rule should apply to your eating plan. Super-foods are potent, concentrated, nutrient dense foods that can boost the immune system, lower inflammation, and enhance overall health and longevity. The following is my suggested list of the top 5 easily available, versatile super-foods:

- *Cacao* (raw chocolate) in the form of a powder or nibs. According to David Wolfe, raw foodist, cacao is the number one source of antioxidants ranking higher than blueberries, green tea, and red wine. Rich in magnesium, manganese, chromium, and iron, this super-food improves cardiovascular health and improves overall mood and energy. Bake with it, sprinkle on top of a morning grain, stir into your coffee, or mix into a smoothie.

- *Maca* powder contains significant amounts of amino acids, carbohydrates, minerals, and vitamins. In powder form, you can bake with this adaptogenic super-food or add to a smoothie.

- *Gogi Berries*, used in traditional Chinese medicine, contains 18 kinds of amino acids, including 8 essential amino acids, a high antioxidant content, trace minerals, iron, and vitamins as well as many other nutrients. Bake with it or add it to your morning cereal or grain. It is less sweet than raisins or dried cranberries and may take a little getting used to.

- The three power seeds: *hemp*, *chia*, and *flax*. High protein sources and rich in iron, vitamin E, and anti-inflammatory omega-3 fatty acids, these seeds taste great and make a nutritious addition to almost any dish from cereal to salad to any kind of burger.

- Other super-food options include *spirulina*, *blue green algae*, *chlorella*, *wheatgrass*, or any of the commercial green super-food powder mixtures, *bee pollen*, *acai berry* and *camu berry* powder, sea vegetables, and medicinal mushrooms. For purposes of this book, I won't go into the specific benefits of each, but they are worth investigating for overall health and wellness.

7. Keep processed foods to a minimum. Avoid white flour, white sugar, white salt, trans fats, refined, processed foods, and high fructose corn syrup in particular.

8. Make small changes slowly. Changing your eating habits takes patience. It is a process like anything else. Examine what you eat and find one or two areas where you can make small improvements that will stick. Go slowly and allow your body to adjust.

Recovery Nutrition:

Meals. Here is where the real fun starts. While rest days are a vital part of any training plan, so too are recovery meals, especially after those long runs. Food tastes great and should be enjoyed, but food serves a functional purpose as well. By manipulating what you eat, you can not only run faster, stronger, and longer, but you can help your body recover sooner.

When? Remember the above guideline to eat when you are hungry. Well, here is the exception to that rule. Many scientific studies show that recovery begins within 30 minutes following prolonged exercise. Eating within 35-60 minutes of your long run will help your body begin to replenish depleted glycogen stores and repair muscle tissue.

What? To replace glycogen and repair muscle tissue, choose a mix of simple carbohydrates and protein. Many sources will tell you to choose a mix of carbohydrates and protein in a 3:1 or 4:1 (carbohydrates to protein) ratio. Within this ratio, you are supposed to aim for approximately 0.5 grams of carbohydrate per pound of body weight combined with approximately 15-25 grams of protein. What??? Hopefully running will become a lasting part of your life as well as healthy, clean eating. To make this goal a reality, let's keep it simple. Nobody eats according to burdensome rules, ratios, & formulas, at least, not for long. It is not practical and it is not fun. Hummus and spouted bread, cottage cheese and fruit, Greek yogurt and a handful of trail mix, or almond butter and a banana are all good examples of a recovery snack. Many runners, myself included, do not feel particularly hungry after a long run. If that is the case, a drink that includes protein and carbohydrates is a good choice. For the runner with the sensitive stomach, drinks are not only easier to digest, but offer the hydration that is so crucial after a long training session. Chocolate milk seems to be a favorite among many runners. Compared to plain milk, water, or most sugary sports drinks, it has a 2:1 carbohydrate to protein

content along with calcium. I personally avoid chocolate milk and gravitate towards custom made
smoothies that are lower in sugar and can be tweaked
to my own personal tastes and nutritional needs. In
fact, I rely heavily on smoothies during my training
and encourage you to do so as well. Smoothies are
easy to make. A blender and some simple ingredients
are all you need.

Adina's Recovery Smoothie

- Liquid base. Begin with your choice of 1 cup coconut water, low fat milk or any milk substitute
  from store bought soy to homemade cashew
  milk. My personal preference is a store bought
  almond milk. Choose unsweetened milk substi-
  tutes that do not contain carageenan.

- Add your fruit. I use 1 frozen banana plus about
  a cup or handful of frozen berries. I like to use
  berries for their antioxidant and anti-
  inflammatory benefits, but any fruit will do. You
  can use fresh fruit as well, but I prefer frozen as it
  produces a thicker liquid.

- Power it up. Add a few of the super foods listed
  above. My personal favorites are one tablespoon
  raw cacao powder, one tablespoon flax seed, and
  one scoop of Amazing Grass green super-food
  powder or a handful of fresh or frozen dark

greens like kale, spinach, beet greens, collards, or chard. You will need to experiment here to make this your own. Also, if you are using a milk with a low protein profile, such as almond milk, add some form of protein here such as Greek yogurt, a whey protein powder, nut butter, or one of the three power seeds.

• Other options. Depending on your tastes, you may choose to add a fat (if you have not added a nut butter) in the form of coconut oil or avocado or you may choose to sweeten your smoothie with dates, stevia, or one of the many natural sweeteners available to you. You may also want to add vanilla or almond extract depending on what you have already included.

Two more important notes about post recovery nutrition. Research shows that the anabolic boost stimulated by a single dose of amino acids is transient and lasts only one to two hours. In other words, do not consume all your protein at once. Be conscious of including protein for muscle recovery and spread it out over the course of your day, particularly the 24 hours following your long run. Continue to incorporate carbohydrates throughout the day with the focus now shifting from simple to complex carbs. To increase your body's natural healing abilities, include as many anti-inflammatory foods as possible.

Supplements:

Vitamin C, a water soluble vitamin and powerful antioxidant, is helpful during and after training when your body is under stress and your immune system is more susceptible. The National Institute of Health (NIH) recommends a daily intake of 90 mg. vitamin C per day for men and 75 mg. per day for women. Dr. Andrew Weil states that for most healthy individuals, the body can only hold and use about 250mg of vitamin C a day, and any excess is lost though urine. At times of illness, during recovery from injury, or under conditions of increased oxidative stress, i.e. training for and running a marathon, the body can use greater amounts. I take 500 mg. per day when training. I feel that this is enough to boost immunity, certainly not enough to cause an imbalance, and easy to take in one tablet.

I will briefly mention **Vitamin D** because many individuals are deficient in this important vitamin which influences the development of your immune cells. Our body doesn't make vitamin D on its own, but creates the precursor to it, referred to as vitamin D2. When we get ultraviolet exposure, that precursor is made and then converted, by the liver and kidney, to the active form of vitamin D. If you are not getting enough sun exposure from all those training runs (or are wearing sun block) and a blood test shows that you are vitamin D deficient, you will probably need to add a supplement to your regimen.

Some runners use additional supplements such as branch chain amino acids (leucine, isoleucine and va-line) and L-Glutamine to aid in muscle repair and boost athletic performance. I have never felt the need to use these and cannot vouch for their effectiveness.

There are a multitude of herbs and many spices that have anti-inflammatory effects that are essential to speed post workout recovery. Turmeric, chili peppers, basil, cinnamon, and ginger are just a few of the many spices and herbs available to liberally use in your daily cooking regimen. Including these in your diet will enhance the flavor of food, improve overall health, and speed recovery.

Just the long run?

I specify a recovery regimen following the long run, but it is important to note two things. Any speed training can be as equally grueling as a long run and requires the same post care and attention. Also note

that any workout may be more strenuous for a beginning runner than a more experienced, efficient
runner. It is important to assess your workout level
and be aware of what you are eating throughout the
course of any training program.

Recovery Hydration:

Here, again, there is a lot of advice for drinking the
correct amount of fluid to rehydrate. Some say to aim
for 16-20 ounces of fluid and continue hydrating
with eight or more ounces every half hour for two to
six hours. Very precise. Others recommend 2.5 cups
of fluid for each pound of body weight lost. And yet
others say drink half your body weight in ounces daily. The amount of liquid you consume is contingent
on so many different variables that I prefer a more
intuitive approach and like the advice of Tim Noakes,
M.D., author of Waterlogged: The Serious Problem
of over-hydration in Endurance Sports, who relies on
the body's thirst mechanism to signal when and how
much to hydrate. I am not underestimating the importance of rehydrating with water or with an
electrolyte drink (I use Nuun tablets), but there is a
balance that each runner must personally achieve
based on their individual biochemistry. You can
judge whether your hydration practices are adequate
by looking at the color of your urine. If your urine is

a pale yellow, you are adequately hydrated. If it is clear, you are drinking too much and if it is dark, you are not drinking enough. Looking at your face and clothes to see if they are coated with grainy, white streaks (as well as paying attention to cravings) is another good way to judge whether you need to replace lost sodium as well. Staying away from dehydrating liquids like coffee and alcohol might also help when trying to rehydrate. Remember, keep it simple and be attuned to what your body is telling you.

Race Day:

Before: Pre-race breakfast. This is totally individual and something that needs to be experimented with and established well before race day. The best pre-race breakfast consists mainly of carbohydrates since they are digested most rapidly and are your body's preferred source of fuel. Small amounts of protein will keep you satisfied longer, but you may want to avoid fat which takes a while to digest. Fiber is your friend but maybe not so much on race day. You may want to limit this to avoid possible bloating and GI problems. Meals that include dairy or a lot of sugar may also irritate some stomachs and lead to diarrhea, otherwise known as "runner's trots", so be aware of what you are eating and how you react during your training runs.

Sources say that the ideal pre-race breakfast consists of 1.5 to 1.8 grams of carbohydrate per pound of body weight 3 to 4 hours before the race. This is way too many carbs for me to comfortably digest at way too early an hour in the morning. I do not follow this rule nor do the runners that I know. Overloading your system with more carbs and liquid than you can comfortably handle may lead to digestive problems. A general guideline is to have half of your carbohydrate load about two hours before the race and then an easily digestible, high carbohydrate snack about thirty minutes before start time. As a side note, if you reek of ammonia after a long run, your body might be lacking an adequate amount of carbohydrates to fuel your run. When you do not have enough carbs to support a run, your body will burn protein for fuel. It will break down the amino acids that make up protein and convert it into glucose. Within these amino acids is nitrogen. When too much nitrogen is present in your system, your kidneys process the excess. This process creates urea, which is expelled through your urine. However, when there is too much for the kidneys to process, then the excess nitrogen is secreted as ammonia through your sweat. If your sweat smells like ammonia, try to increase your carbohydrates. If this doesn't do the trick, it might just be that your sweat naturally smells like ammonia, which is a natural by-product of heavy exercise and perspiration. Drinking more water while you exercise might dilute the ammonia and minimize the odor. If neither what you eat nor what you drink has any effect, see your doctor to rule out an electrolyte imbalance or liver or kidney damage. Again, choosing a plan that works for you by experimenting during training is essential.

During: Fueling On the Go. Again, individual, individual, individual and experiment, experiment, experiment! During cooler months, I alternate between water and a cornstarch energy drink every mile with eating anything from an energy chew (my favorite is Cliff shots) to half a banana every third mile. I also like a caffeine energy strip before race time and then at every hour mark. This is my general framework which I tweak depending on weather, my speed, and simply how I am feeling. It works for me, but may not work for you. There are so many performance enhancing supplements from gels and chews to caffeine, creatine, beet juice and beta alanine. Bite size pieces of natural foods can also enhance performance and are used by many amateur and professional runners. It is about finding what works for you. That may be a process that spans several racing seasons.

The only hard set advice that I can offer here is to avoid chugging too much water. Not only does it make you bloated, but it can dilute your electrolytes and cause abnormally low sodium levels. This, in turn, can cause muscle weakness, cramping and, in extreme cases, hyponatremia, a life threatening condition. The key is to stay well hydrated well before race day while finding the right amount of liquid that works for you. The other hard and fast rule is to stick with what works and do not experiment on race day. Your training runs are your dress rehearsals. It is the time to figure out what fuels you most effectively and what triggers discomfort.

I wish you all happy, healthy, safe, and energized running!

Adina Kelman
Holistic Health Coach

If you would like to contact Adina directly, you may do so! Here's how:

Website: **www.alifeinbalance.co**
Email: **adinakelman@alifeinbalance.co**

To leave comments or questions about this chapter on the website, go to this chapter on:

www.YouCanGoTheDistance.com/book

Let the Taper Begin!

I have to confess that tapering is one of the hardest parts of my marathon training.

I have been training hard for 15 weeks and now the race is only 3 weeks away. My mind wants to push just a little harder and go just a little farther to insure I am in peak condition, but my body desperately wants a break!

Here is an excerpt from one of my blog posts as I began a taper:

You see, there are two conflicting processes happening in me right now. Last Friday, I went out for my last 20 mile run. It did not go as well as I had hoped and I wound up running it slower than I had planned and I was exhausted at the end. Not a good sign.

Because my last long run wasn't as strong as I wanted, there is a part of my brain that tells me I need to get out there and try it again and push a little harder. That is my ego talking!

However, because it did not go as well as I had hoped, I know my body is telling me that it is time to start backing off and giving it time to recover so I can be fully rested come race day.

It's time to listen to my body!

Tapering is a critical part of marathon training!

I wrote in a previous chapter about how important Long Run Recovery is.

Basically, we need to think of all of the weeks of training that have led up to this week as one very long Long Run. Now it is time to give our bodies some well needed recovery time!

Pre-race jitters will start to set in at this point and you will start to question if you have done all you could, over the last 15 weeks, to prepare yourself for the marathon. You will start to wonder if you are really ready. Let me assure you this feeling is natural and even the most seasoned marathoners go through the same emotional questioning before each race.

If you are getting really tired, your performance is starting to decline, and you have a few nagging aches that just will not go away, it is time to listen to your body.

That is why we need to taper! We are worn out at this point in our training and we need to recover!

The goal of the taper is to spend the next 3 weeks allowing your body to rest, repair the little micro-tears that have developed in our muscles and rebuild the nutrients we are going to need come race day. Without a 3-week taper, those things will not happen and your performance will suffer.

The problem with the taper is all mental! Every time I get to this point, I start to doubt my training and I wonder if I will lose my conditioning if I back off. However, I know from experience just the opposite is true. You will not lose any conditioning. In fact, it will help!

Here is a little secret most runners do not know: *You can go a full 2 weeks without running at all and not lose your conditioning!*

You need to repeat to yourself these mantras: "we build strength while resting, not while running!" and "it is better to go into a marathon a little under-conditioned than to push too hard and get injured!"

Do not misunderstand the taper! Tapering is not bringing your training to a complete stop! It is about backing it down gradually so you can get in the rest and recovery you need.

So what does my taper plan look like? With three weeks before my race, it looks like this:

Last weekend, I did the last (of 4) 20-mile Long Runs. This weekend, I will go 13 and then only 8 the weekend after that. Meanwhile, this week and next, I will continue to do my mid-week speed (Yasso 800s) and Tempo Runs, but they will also be shorter and a bit slower.

During the final week leading up the race, I will only go out for an easy 4-mile run at Race Pace.

Also, during these taper weeks, I will be trying to go to bed a little earlier than usual, hoping to bank some rest. I know that a few days before the race, I will be getting nervous and not sleeping as well, so I will try to catch up on sleep now!

I will also be eating well. During these next 3 weeks, you should be thinking about healthy food choices. Your body will need the fuel storage come race day. Refer to the chapter, *Nutrition: Choose the Right Fuels!*, for a more detailed discussion on food choices.

My goal for the next 3 weeks is to try to relax, trust my training, and rest enough to allow my body time to get rid of the nagging aches that have been around for a few weeks. I want to go into the race without any sore muscles!

I hope your training has gone well and that you will trust it enough to back off and get some much needed recovery time. The race is only 3 weeks away! Relax and have fun!

To leave comments or questions about this chapter on the website, go to this chapter on:

www.YouCanGoTheDistance.com/book

Ready or Not, It's GO Time!

Well, you have trained hard for the last 16 to 20 weeks and it is finally here: Race Week!

If you have made it this far, you are already a champion! No matter how the race goes at the end of this week, you are a winner!

This is the week you have been training for, so it is time to relax, trust the training and mentally prepare for this coming weekend!

Here are some things that you should NOT do this week:

- Do not try any new foods or drinks—eat/drink only what has been working for you!
- Do not go buy new shoes, shorts, or shirts—run in what you have trained in!
- Do not try to get in any kind of workout other than walks or very light jogs—you need the rest!
- Do not go roller-skating, play soccer or any other sport—do not risk any injuries!
- Do not second guess your training! Stay positive!

Here are some things that you SHOULD do this week:

- Get extra sleep. Start going to bed early and sleeping later than usual—you will not sleep well the night before the race, so get your sleep in the bank now!

- Stay off your feet as much as possible.

- Drink, drink, drink! Start hydrating now. Drink more water than you normally do. Carry a water bottle around with you everywhere you go so you do not forget!

- Eat well. Try to avoid fatty foods. Get in a good balance of carbs and proteins.

- Trim your toenails today if they need it! Seriously! do not wait until the night before and risk trimming them too short so they hurt during the run!

- Start watching the weather forecast and planning what to wear on race morning (nothing new!)

- Gather up all of your running gear and put it all in one place so you aren't hunting for it the night before.

- If you run with a GPS watch, charge it up!

- Go through a mental run-through of your race and know where you should be on the course at certain times.

- Be very positive! This is a mental race just as much, if not more, than a physical race. Your mind controls your muscles, so get rid of any negative thoughts or doubts. Talk to yourself as if you've already run the race and it went great!

- Almost all races have pace group leaders. Decide now if you are going to run with the group for your planned pace or just go it on your own. I highly recommend you go with the pace group because you'll be running with runners with the same goals and you can motivate each other along the way.

- If your race has a big Expo as part of the packet pickup process, go and mingle—be part of the community.

- If your race offers a bus tour of the race, go on the tour to familiarize yourself with the hills at specific mile markers—make a mental plan for dealing with them.

- Figure out exactly how you are getting to the race, how long it will take to get there, where you are going to park, who will meet you along the course (and where), who will meet you at the finish, etc.

- Plan to be at the starting line no less than 30 minutes before the race starts!

Here are some things to do on the morning of your race:

- Get up early enough so you do not have to rush to get out the door.

- As soon as you get up, drink as much water as you can.

- Continue drinking until about 45 minutes before the race and then do not drink any more.

- Get to the starting area early enough to use the facilities to empty your bladder just before the race starts—very important!

- Eat whatever you have eaten before your other Long Runs and NOTHING new!

- Say to yourself: I can do this! I CAN go the distance!

Race Start Tip: The best tip I can give you is: do NOT go out too fast!

Going out too fast is something that can happen without you even knowing it because you are so excited and just moving along with the crowd! In one race, my planned race pace was 8:00 minutes per mile. After 2 miles into the race, I glanced at my GPS watch and realized I was running a 6:45 pace! I had no idea. I felt good and I was just keeping up with the flow of runners. Nevertheless, I slammed on the brakes and let lots of people pass me. I'm so glad I did, because I passed most of them later in the race.

Remember to run your race according to your plan, not according to the pace of the crowd.

I am not going to wish you good luck because you do not need luck! You have planned and trained. Now, you just need to execute that plan.

I will tell you this: Have fun and remember to smile and wave to everyone with a camera!

To leave comments or questions about this chapter on the website, go to this chapter on:

www.YouCanGoTheDistance.com/book

The Finish Line!

Congratulations, you did it! You have crossed the finish line!

It has been a long, enjoyable journey and your marathon training paid off.

For me, there are not many things more satisfying than the feeling I get every time I cross the finish line of a marathon. It is an exhilarating feeling of accomplishment! Regardless of how I feel, physically, or how well I performed in regard to my goal, the satisfaction of crossing that line after running 26.2 miles is one of the best feelings in the world!

No matter how close you came to your time goal, you should be very proud of yourself. You are now a member of a very exclusive club. You are now a Marathon Runner. Less than 1% of the people who live on this planet can make that claim!

One of the first things I would like you to do is to tell the world about your accomplishment. Post your accomplishment on all of the social media platforms. Put in on Facebook, LinkedIn, Twitter, etc. Tell the world what you did. It is perfectly OK to boast about this achievement and you deserve some applause.

Let me help you spread the word. Send a Tweet with your race name and time and I will share with my followers:

www.twitter.com/YouCanGoTheDist

Share your accomplishment with other readers by posting about your experience on the website. Runners, more than any group of people I know, love to hear about the success of other runners! You can share with us here:

www.YouCanGoTheDistance.com/book/finish-line

Let me share with you the story of one of my last marathons, the Richmond Marathon on November 10, 2012:

My goal for the 2012 Richmond Marathon was to finish in 3:30:00 (3 hours and 30 minutes) and, at the age of 49, would qualify me for the Boston Marathon.

I will spare you the suspense and say that I did not hit that goal. I completed the marathon in 3:50:37, but I am still very pleased with that result!

I am still pleased with the result because of something that I was able to accomplish that is often harder than the physical effort required to run a marathon. I won a major mental battle! I was able to fight off the feelings of disappointment and depression and was able to reset my goal mid-race.

I started the race very intentionally watching my pace to make sure I did not go out too fast!

While it still feels awkward every time I do it, I used Jeff Galloway's run/walk/run method throughout the race. This means I ran at a 7:45 pace for 2 miles and then walked for 30 seconds, keeping my pace at a 8:00 average.

At 10K, I was feeling great. I crossed the 10K timing mat at 49:25, which was a 7:57 pace and slightly ahead of my goal.

I crossed the 13.1 mile timing mat in 1:45:05, an average 8:01 pace. I was still very pleased with that time given the significant hills I had just come through.

While I was trying to "race" the marathon and to maintain my target pace, I had a very important stop to make at mile 14.

My mother and my youngest son, Carter, came down to cheer for me along the route and they were there to greet me at mile 14.

Even though my mother encouraged me to keep going and just wave to them, there was no way I was going to run past my boy without stopping to give him a big hug and kiss, and that is exactly what I did!

The stop cost me about 15 seconds, but the look of happiness on my son's face, knowing his daddy loved him enough to stop for a hug, gave me the emotional boost to make up the time and I still ran that mile in 7:46!

Captain, We Have a Problem!

While training for this race, I developed a Morton's Neuroma in my right foot. Although it was painful, I trained through it and hoped for the best. During the race, however, I must have been compensating for it more than I thought and, 16 miles into the race, my left knee started to get very sore!

Just before mile 18, I stumbled and my left knee buckled underneath me and I knew the "race" was over. Nevertheless, I was pretty sure my knee would hold up for the rest of the course, but not at the pace I was going.

Mid-Race Goal/Attitude Adjustments

As I walked into the water station at mile 18, I knew I had to make a choice about the rest of the course.

The way I saw it, I had three choices: I could quit and get a ride back to the finish area; I could continue to run and try to get as close to my goal as possible despite the pain or risk of injury; or I could just let go of the goal, relax, and finish the run at any easy pace, enjoying the fans, bands and beautiful weather.

I chose to let go, relax, and just enjoy myself!

I must admit it took me another two miles before I was able to shake off the disappointment and rearrange my attitude.

The crowd made the difference! Even though my knee was throbbing and I was walking more than jogging, there were scores of people on the side of the road cheering for me and encouraging me to keep going. There were smiling kids with their hands out asking for Hi-Fives as I passed by. How can you not keeping going with that kind of encouragement?

So, with a new goal of just having fun and enjoying the crowd, the sights, the sounds and the gorgeous mid-60 degree weather, I set back into a steady jog.

The rest of the marathon was spent with a smile, and the occasional grimace of pain on my face and a new sense of satisfaction that, even though I would not reach my initial goal, I would be able to overcome the potentially biggest obstacle we face: *a bad attitude.*

Perhaps the most satisfying thing that has ever happened to me during a marathon happened at mile 24, with just 2.1 miles left to go in the race.

I jogged up behind a lady who was walking and crying. I stopped, walked along beside her and asked her what was wrong. (Please keep in mind that during a marathon, your brain can really play tricks on you and you can become, literally, disoriented to your place and time.) Sobbing, she said that she, too, had been trying to qualify for Boston but had run out of steam a few miles back. She was so disappointed in herself and I knew that feeling.

I asked her more questions about her time goal and it dawned on me she had absolutely no idea how close she was to the finish line! We only had 2.1 miles to go and she had 19 minutes to cover that distance and still reach her goal. When I told her this, she didn't believe me. I showed her the mile marker we just past and the time on her watch. Her face lit up and she said "do you think I can do it?" I said, "I think you can! It is sure worth a try!"

I stayed with her and we started jogging again. There were a few more times she wanted to stop, but I encouraged her to keep going. Once we rounded the last corner in downtown Richmond, we could see the finish line and it was all downhill. "You're going to make it!" I said to her and pointed to the finish banner!

She crossed the finish line and qualified for the Boston Marathon with 12 seconds to spare! I was so proud of her! Her family was waiting there for her and I lost her in the crowd. I never even learned her name, but my heart was so happy for her!

As for me, I crossed the finish line with a time of 3:50:37, 20 minutes shy of my Boston goal, but I had accomplished something more. To help someone else reach their goal is, for me, a much more fulfilling thing!

As an added bonus, who should be the very first person I recognized in the crowd at the finish line?

That's right, the man himself, Bart Yasso (of Yasso 800s fame!). I reached out my sweaty hand to give him a handshake but he would have no part of that. Bart pulled me in for a big bear hug and said "Great job. You rock!"

Any chance of disappointment creeping back into my brain was crushed by Bart's hug and encouraging words! Thanks, Bart! You rock too!

So there you have it. My 2012 Richmond Marathon experience!

Thank you for reading my book! I hope I have helped you realize that you CAN go the distance! All you need to do is try!

Again, I would love for you to share your marathon story with us on the website:

www.YouCanGoTheDistance.com/book/finish-line

About the Author

Bruce Van Horn, author of You CAN Go the Distance!, is a writer, runner, coach, speaker, and business owner. He lives with his family in the Richmond, Virginia area.

Bruce has a heart for coaching and encouraging people to overcome their fears and self-doubt, live intentionally, passionately, and achieve goals they never thought possible.

Follow Bruce on his website, Twitter or Facebook:

Website: **www.brucevanhorn.com**
Twitter: **www.twitter.com/brucevh**
Facebook: **www.facebook.com/brucevh**

The YCGTD Training Plan

Throughout the book, I reference the YCGTD Marathon Training Plan. Here are the details of the plan.

The plan is very easy to follow and can be used for first-timers and advanced marathoners alike.

The plan simply uses three core workouts, as described in the book:

- Yasso 800s
- Tempo Runs
- Long Runs

The first thing you need before you can start using the Training Plan is a goal. You need to have a goal for how fast you want to run your marathon. For help on deciding your goal, read the chapter **First Things First: Set A Goal.**

Once you have your Marathon Goal, you need to know what that goal breaks down to in Minutes per Mile. For example, to run a 4-hour marathon, that would be a 9:10 pace (9 minutes, 10 seconds, per mile). We refer that that pace as your Race Pace, or "RP" for short.

With those two numbers, your Marathon Goal and Race Pace, you now have what you need for determining how fast (or slow) to do your core workouts. Now it's just a matter of following the plan!

The YCGTD Marathon Training Plan only has 3 running days per week. The other days are Cross-Training or Rest days. A typical week might look like this:

- Sun: Rest
- Mon: Rest
- Tue: Yasso 800s
- Wed: Cross-Train
- Thu: Tempo Run
- Fri: Cross-Train
- Sat: Long Run

Of course, you can modify your workouts to suit your schedule, but I do recommend having a Cross-Training or Rest day in between the core workout days.

This, and all Marathon Training plans, assumes that you have done your Foundation training and are in good enough shape to start Week 1. If not, read the chapter **Build a Strong Foundation**, before you begin.

Use this worksheet and the Training Schedule on the next page to guide you through your training:

Marathon Goal: _____ (hh:mm:ss)

Yasso 800s time: _____ (mm:ss, based on Marathon Goal)

Race Pace (RP): _____ (mm:ss per mile, based on Marathon Goal)

On the Training Schedule, you will see the miles you should run each week, and the pace at which you should run them. Note that the +/- numbers indicate the number of seconds you should add to or subtract from your pace. For example, if your RP is 10:00 per mile, on Week 1, your Tempo Run is 3 miles at 9:30 (RP – 30 seconds) and your Long Run is 8 miles at 11:00 (RP + 60 seconds)

To view/download a printable copy of the YCGTD Marathon Training Plan, go to:

www.YouCanGoTheDistance.com/Plan

Training Schedule

Week #	Yasso 800s	Tempo Run	Long Run
18	2x	3 mi @ RP - 30	8 mi @ RP + 60
17	2x	5 mi @ RP - 30	10 mi @ RP + 60
16	3x	7 mi @ RP - 30	13 mi @ RP + 60
15	3x	7 mi @ RP - 30	15 mi @ RP + 60
14	4x	9 mi @ RP - 30	18 mi @ RP + 60
13	4x	5 mi @ RP - 40	18 mi @ RP + 45
12	5x	7 mi @ RP - 30	20 mi @ RP + 90
11	5x	7 mi @ RP - 40	15 mi @ RP + 60
10	6x	9 mi @ RP - 30	18 mi @ RP + 45
9	6x	7 mi @ RP - 30	20 mi @ RP + 90
8	7x	10 mi @ RP - 30	13 mi @ RP + 30
7	7x	10 mi @ RP - 30	15 mi @ RP + 30
6	8x	7 mi @ RP - 40	20 mi @ RP + 60
5	9x	8 mi @ RP - 30	15 mi @ RP + 15
4	10x	6 mi @ RP - 40	20 mi @ RP + 60
3	6x	6 mi @ RP - 30	13 mi @ RP
2	4x	6 mi @ RP - 15	8 mi @ RP
Race Week	REST	4 mi @ RP	Marathon Day!

Made in the USA
Lexington, KY
14 September 2014